THE ART OF PASS | FAIL

THE ART OF

OVERCOMING OBJECTIONS
CUSTOMER MANAGEMENT

PASS
FAIL

HOW TO PERSUADE OTHERS AND MAXIMIZE YOUR LIFE

STEVEN E. SHAW

Overcoming Objections
&
Customer Management

The Art of
PASS — FAIL

How to persuade others and maximize your life

Copyright © 2022

All rights reserved. No part of this publication may be reproduced, distributed, or transmitted in any form or by any means, including photocopying, recording, or other electronic or mechanical methods, without the prior written permission of the publisher, except in the case of brief quotations embodied in critical reviews and certain other noncommercial uses permitted by copyright law.

For permission requests, write to the publisher, addressed "Attention: Permissions Coordinator" at the address below.

Steven E. Shaw
Steve@SteveShawTraining.com

ISBN 979-8-9873679-0-2 (hc)
ISBN 979-8-9873679-1-9 (epub)

Printed in the U.S.A

"I understand."

"OH NO YOU DON'T!"

"I'm sorry."

"GO AWAY...
WHY DID YOU DO IT THEN?!?"

Foreword

I salute everyone in advance for your time study. You are to be commended for breaking boundaries and pushing frontiers. You are the ones who make humans worth studying. You are the ones who will prosper for all days to come. I acknowledge those who made this work possible, my friends, colleagues, parents and family. The most special people of influence are ... Stacey Xenides the greatest in graphic design, website and IT, Bryan Shaw who does graphics and digital, Bob Shaw and my parents who are always there showing support.

I require myself to say a few words of sincere thanks to all my friends and family of colleagues out there. You have done so much in inspire me and demand that I deliver the best to you. I believe your success moves me to be the best because you are so driven. I owe it to you to bring the best to you as a friend in life and partner in training. In no order of importance I recognize: Father Bob and Brenda Cawley, Rick Strifler, James Gross, Ron Kiepke, Jeff Zwerling, John Kerley, Jeff Pister, Art Curtis, Jimmy Powell, Jamie Powers, Michael Wright, Chris and Michelle St Peters, Mark and Maria Campbell, Brian Trigalet, Will Rasmussen, Mo Escobar, Roger

The Art of PASS - FAIL

Funston, Mark Rehkopf, Wes Blair, Greg Thornton, Terry Chechakli, Kathy Kimmel, Tamila Bauer, Dave Rogers, Mike VanBrunt, Tom Koshko, Mike Murphy, Travis Maroules, Jamie Powers, Brandon Malatino, Rick Zellers, Anthony Winnigham, Kathy Rocks, Rob Sneed, Jeff Dohallow, Howard Boughter, Eric Langley, Mike Fitzgerald, Kat Gold, Jim Roche, Eric Hart, Marie Knight, Jim Revas III, Steve Schoener, Amy Davis and team, and of course Cindy Lawrence who is an inspiration to so many. Finally, I want to thank the hundreds of teams I have the pleasure of working, creating, and developing together. There are so many special people that I am sure I left some off the list, accidentally of course. I love you all and appreciate your contributions to my life. I hope this book changes everyone's world for the better...

—*Steve Shaw*

Contents

Foreword vii

1 PASS-FAIL: THE ONLY WAY 1
2 Buying Motives 13
3 L.E.A.D Approach to Objection Handling 23
4 Keys to Communication 33
5 Step-By-Step - Listen 55
6 Step-By-Step - Empathize 79
7 Step-By-Step - Ask Clarifying Questions 93
8 Step-By-Step - Determine Solution 107
9 Direct Approach - Consequences 109
10 Return Policy 121
11 L.E.A.D. Customer-Handling Management 125

Maximizing your Life - Beyond the Book 147

PASS-FAIL: THE ONLY WAY

&@*$ You! That's how it all starts. "Your (insert product, store, service) sucks. I want a complete refund for my purchase."

As the wheels turn in your brain, you, the sales representative, begin to realize this is what all the training has been directed toward. Wait! You have not been trained on how to handle a hostile customer? That means you rely on your experience, what you have witnessed, or you simply wing it! The next words to come out of your mouth will decide your day, the customer's day, your company's reputation, and, quite frankly, a lot of paperwork. Next, there may be a management coaching discussion, which could either mean you are fired or, if possible, congratulated.

Well, no one ever gets congratulated on handling an upset customer because that customer is happy and goes on about their business.

In an instant, your brain begrudgingly allows your mouth to open.

What word will you choose? Diffusion or Da Bomb?

Umm, I understand how you feel! **KABOOM!**

I am sorry! **Double KABOOM!**

Please control your language! **Nuclear KABOOM!**

HAHA!

The tweets are now flying. Social media is blowing up. The big boss is calling! This cannot be happening! Oh yes, this is happening now.

In your mind, you may be saying a number of things. *I was just trying to be nice. I was just letting the customer know how much I understand. I wanted to apologize to make the customer feel good. I wanted the customer to know that I cared. The customer is just a complete idiot.* Insert every foul expletive that comes to mind. Really, is it the customer who is a complete jerk, nutjob, or psycho, or is it that most people are not skilled in handling hostile customers?

You may be wondering why I use such coarse language in this introduction. And yes, I toned the language down. Your customer will not. This is the real world. Get over it! People who call customer service lines are not going to be cordial or nice. People who call customer service and complain are not polite. If they were, we could all have ice cream and cookies at work. Customers have an agenda, and the scheme is your company wallet. They want free food, free repairs, and money back after the service is complete or the product is completely used.

This is war. Are you prepared to win? Are you prepared to save your company pocketbook? I realize it is not politically correct to say customer service is war. We are usually told that the customer is always right or to abide by the golden rule: treat everyone the way you want to be treated. But winning the war means defusing the bomb before it goes off, a.k.a. keeping your money and winning the customer.

The Art of PASS - FAIL

Often there are times to retreat and pay the money; however, that is when you raise the flag of defeat. What is your return policy? Does that matter at this point? Ultimately, if the company is wrong, we may simply pay out the cash and move on. The cost is just not worth it. In many cases, the company is what caused the bomb in the first place.

The bomb is the customer service representative who mishandled the customer. The bomb is saying you understand instead of demonstrating understanding. The bomb is sharing an empty "sorry" and making excuses. The nuclear bomb is telling the customer to stop f-ing cussing! When was the last time someone told you to stop doing something and you actually followed the instruction? Out of spite, I will raise my voice when you tell me to be quiet. Out of malice, I will tell you to eff off. Can you handle it? Or will you run and hang up? I own you when you hang up on me! Now you are the problem, not me (the jerk customer).

Social media is the hangout of every person who is scared to talk in person. They are keyboard warriors. This battle you cannot win. That post is online forever. Good luck with getting the customer to retract it. Oh sure, you can get lots of likes, but the message is out there—***You Suck!***

Not only do you suck, but the product also sucks. You suck at customer skills, and you suck at customer resolution. Most likely, you suck at sales too.

Anyone can make a presentation and hope someone makes a purchase. In many cases, the sale simply happens when the customer calls in for a product, service, or repair. Gee! Great job for taking my order.

- My car broke down, and you sold me a widget to fix it. Please, that was me placing an order.
- I need cable TV installed. Can I get a basic package? Give me a break. That is taking a hamburger order at the fast-food joint.
- I would like a #2.
- Would you like fries with that? Sales 101.

In almost any profession these days, companies have made it easy for the consumer to make a purchase. My retired mother can take an order. Your little nephew or niece can "sell" lemonade on a 90-degree day to the moms and dads out on a walk or bike ride. The sale starts when a "NO" is given. What do you do when a prospective buyer says "NO"? Many "salespeople" run at the thought of a "NO." Only the best rise to the occasion.

The Art of PASS - FAIL

"NO," thank you, this [_____] costs too much!
"NO," thank you, I am on a budget!
"NO," thank you, I am out of time today!
"NO," thank you, I just want the basic package.
"NO" Way . . . Insert your most heard objection here

My purpose in writing this book is to provide you with a simple tool to meet these difficult customers head-on. I am going to provide you with simple tools in a complex world. The idea is to defuse, resolve, and prevent the coming explosion. The better idea is to move a customer from "NO" to "YES!" The best situation would be for the customer to realize they are being a jerk (not likely) or for the customer to get themselves to a "yes" purchasing situation.

This is what we will do in the following pages. I am going to present the best approach for defusing a hostile customer as well as overcoming any customer objections. The approach we will discuss is called LEAD. This stands for "Listen," "Empathize," "Ask questions," and "Determine solution." This LEAD approach works the same in both hostile customer management and objection handling. As you will see at the end of the material, you will be poised to get more of what you want out of life by mastering this approach.

Steven E. Shaw

Pass-Fail Approach to Everything

Pass-Fail Buying

The salesperson makes the pitch. The salesperson puts forward the best effort to make a sale. At the end of the presentation, there are two possible outcomes: pass or fail. This presentation concludes with the customer providing an answer to the closing question. In fact, I do not care about your sales approach, technique, or presentation style. Find another book for that advice. The sale only ends when the salesperson allows it to end.

Two options exist at this point:

1) Pass
2) Fail

The salesperson passes when the customer says yes! Congratulations. Stop reading here.

The salesperson fails when the customer says "NO." It is a simple concept without nuance. It is not on a scale of one to ten. It is black and white. Stop or go. **Pass or fail.**

The untrained salesperson panics and starts trying to backpedal or force the customer into continuing the conversation. This is a high-pressure tactic. The reason this is high pressure is that the customer has politely said "NO, thank you." Quite often, the prospective customer thinks by saying "NO," the presentation is complete, and you are done.

"NO" = End to the customer.

Another reason this is high pressure is the salesperson does not have permission to continue the presentation. At some point, the salesperson was given an appointment to present the product or permission to make the sales pitch. When the prospective buyer says "NO" to the pitch, that permission has been revoked. In the standard social contract, this is the time to quit—and many do quit.

Quitters do not make sales. Salespersons that quit are just order takers. Can the salesperson have it both ways? Meaning, can we continue presenting if we are told "NO"? Of course! If you have the correct approach to "NO," it is the *art of the sale* that starts at *"NO."* The best sales approach would be to regain permission to continue and present a better case for the purchase.

There are plenty of overused, misused, and misguided approaches to objection handling on the internet. Certainly, many old-school sales techniques are used in objection handling. These failed approaches only lead to heartache and lost sales.

Pass-Fail Customer Management

Imagine your most hostile customer, the nuisance. This person contacts you or your company with a problem. There are only two outcomes in this situation. The associate **passes** when the customer's anger is defused. The problem customer will accept your solution and happily return for future business with you and the organization. The associate **fails** when the situation escalates and the customer leaves, never to return. In our modern world, this person proceeds to their favorite social media platform and drops a bomb on your world.

This is a pass-or-fail world. Pass, and you live happily ever after. Fail, and you are doomed. There is no middle ground. Customers either return, and we pass, or they do not come back, and we fail. I have seen, read, and reviewed surveys, books, and research that grade customer service on a scale. Have you seen grades between one and ten? The facts are that any answer from one to nine is a failing grade. Ten is the only passing grade. For example, look at the "like" and "dislike" buttons on social media. The more "likes" you receive, the more you pass in the court of public opinion.

$$\text{Pass = Like.}$$
$$\text{Fail = Dislike.}$$

It is that simple. Who says, "Rate my post on a scale of one to ten"? No one. A LIKE feeds my ego. Some sites do not even have dislikes. You either pass with a like, or you fail without a like. It is that simple. How do you feel when you post your selfie, your family photo, vacation destination, or whatever you ate for dinner, and then no one "likes" your post? Most people feel like a failure. Your business is in the same situation. You pass with a stellar social media review, or you fail with a social media bomb. In today's world, people consider businesses with no reviews a failure.

"Approach" vs. "Technique"

I like to use the word "approach" versus "technique." An approach is a well-thought-out process for achieving the desired result. This result is a win for all parties.

A technique is a slick sleight of hand to confuse your opponent. This technique is often followed by buyer's remorse and consumer dissatisfaction.

The approach discussed in this book is about how to continue customer relationships and build upon the trust established by allowing the customer to see you as a partner, not an opponent. The goal is to position yourself as their advocate, not an adversary. In any sales process, objections are a normal part of the experience. When a customer has a need, and your product fulfills that requirement, both parties win. The best approach will have the goal of success for all parties as the outcome. You, as the salesperson, are the only one who can deliver this desired result.

The ensuing approach will defuse any negative thoughts, allow the customer's objections to be identified, establish you as the best person to fulfill the customer's needs, and allow the customer to make the final decision to buy from you.

Approach - Well-thought-out process

Technique - Slick sleight of hand. Trick to confuse

Buying Motives

I am often hired to help companies improve their sales. I get questions about how to make the staff better salespeople. The truth is no one can make you a better salesperson. If you want to improve your trade, that takes effort. Improvement takes commitment to the cause.

I learned to surf at a young age, and the best advice I ever got was to get more water time. Spend more time in the water, and I would learn to catch a wave. That sure made sense to me back then. Pilots improve with more flying time and study. Crypto experts become experts by spending their hard-earned Fiat money on blockchain technologies. They research the projects and spend a considerable amount of time on the exchanges. Regardless of the career, it takes time and effort to improve. It takes dedication to your craft to become a master.

If you want to become a master at sales, then you must do the same. You will need to spend time learning your product, researching the competition, and positioning your approach to the prospective buyer. Make no mistake. You will close more deals by learning LEAD. Consider LEAD a tool to create buyers. My job is to share this new tool with you so that your customer wants to give you their money. Use the tools in your toolbox, and allow the customer to give you their money.

The Sales Formula

A sale happens when two important elements come together. These two items are need and value. The sales formula is:

$$Need + Value = Sale$$

Customers in all areas of retail and business transactions generally have only two motives for making a purchase. The concepts I will discuss are called *fear of loss* and *hope for gain*.

Fear of Loss

The first motive that drives a customer to make a purchase is called **fear of loss.** Fear of loss is a concept that suggests that a customer will buy items or services because they are afraid of what could happen if they do not buy the item or service. This concept is not a scare tactic and does not mean you should scare a customer into buying. It simply means that customers themselves have a fear that something could go wrong if they fail to make this purchase right now.

Most customers fear the loss of money. LACK OF MONEY is the ultimate fear for people and businesses alike. I recently read that 78 percent of Americans live paycheck to paycheck. People who live paycheck to paycheck have money, but they have their entire paycheck allocated to other items rather than whatever product or service you are selling.

These people are not good or bad people. They are everyday consumers: husbands, wives, families, and normal folks trying to keep their heads above water. Many people who shop at our stores have bills to pay. These bills include credit cards, mortgages, rent payments, car payments, boat payments, college payments, diapers, cell phones, booze, gambling, etc. What do I pay first? Most likely, it's the oldest bill in the stack. Some people are just trying to keep the lights on and the creditors off their backs.

FEAR of LOSS = NEED

Back to the concept of fear of loss, or, as I call it, NEED. I, the consumer, will buy the items that I need to maintain my lifestyle. If I need something, remember I will buy these needed items to prevent more expenditures in the near future. And "near future" is the key phrase. If I can put it off to a future date, that works even better. I have other bills to pay that are more important. The base of many sales is derived from a simple concept: ***if I need it, I will buy it!*** As I will demonstrate soon, if I need it, I will buy it from you.

Some critics will comment that a "want" is also important. I agree with the critics. That is a need. Other books may define the differences between needs and wants.

For our purposes here, I will continue to combine both. You could argue that Need or Want + Value = Sale.

To be clear, the value is easier to demonstrate if a customer wants an item. A strong want becomes a need. It is easy to blur the lines. I want this item because it makes me feel better. Throughout this material, remember Need + Value = Sale.

Hope for Gain

The concept of **hope for gain** means that a customer will exchange money in hopes of gaining something better than the dollars they are giving away. A customer will give one hundred dollars to a company or a salesperson, hoping the item is worth more than the money given. This idea is called a value proposition. A value proposition states that value must overcome the cost of an item for the sale to be successful.

This concept provokes the idea that when the customer makes a purchase ($100, for example), the returning usefulness is greater than what was paid. The value to me, the customer, is greater than the purchase price or money exchanged.

HOPE FOR GAIN = VALUE

Value can be derived in many ways. Value can be in the form of providing safety or reliability in an automobile. Value can be in the form of protecting my investment via an insurance policy. Value can be in the form of the taste of the steak or wine from the swanky new restaurant in town. Value can be in the form of my ego being stroked because I am wearing the latest fashion or carrying the newest purse.

Imagine spending hundreds of dollars for a weekend at a high-end resort versus staying at a cheap motel. The value of an item is the actual dollar amount a consumer is willing to spend to have that item. The value proposition goes back to the first ancient marketplace where peasants exchanged livestock for clothing or gold coins for food or other essential items.

I propose the concept that the following statement is self-evident: if the consumer comes to your establishment, then the consumer inherently sees the value of your organization. Whether the consumer walks next door or drives across town to shop at your business, a decision was made that you have some value. If the potential client establishes a meeting with you, they see an inherent value in your product or service. It could be the convenience of a local 7-Eleven. It could be the notoriety of Harley Davidson or savings at Costco. If the customer enters your establishment, searches you online, or calls your phone, there is an innate value in you—at that moment.

For example, a Walmart shopper sees the value of discounted prices as a factor in choosing Walmart. Maybe the consumer sees that Walmart has such a selection that this becomes a one-stop shop. That will save them time from running all over town. The time savings could be the value proposition they need to make a purchase. The consumer does not haggle with the check-out person. The consumer makes the selection and pays the price of the item. The value of the item outweighed the cost, and a transaction was completed.

Let us use a hardware store as another example. The customer walks into the store to make a purchase of necessary home repair supplies. It is self-evident that the customer sees value in the hardware store. The customer picked that store to shop in. The hardware store has the right supplies, tools, and home repair items. The customer makes the purchase. The value proposition has been executed. The customer gave money in return for supplies and tools *needed* that are seen as having a greater value than the money given. The value has exceeded the cost, and a sale is completed.

The job of management and owners is to create a brand image to present to the customer. The brand image of the establishment via its marketing is what drives the consumer into the store. The job of the sales consultant is only to create the need (want, desire) in the customer. This need is what completes the purchase. Need + Value = Sale.

For years, sales training focused on creating value. Value is the second half of the equation. The theory presented here is that the value in products and services is typically created when the customer chooses to walk in or log on and buy an item, product, or service. The focus of this book is to give the salesperson the tools to complete the sale. Create a need, desire, or want, and allow a customer to buy the items they want from your company.

Problem-Solving Salespeople

Most salespersons have a knack for solving problems. The best can move and dance in a conversation, quickly find solutions for the customer, and provide answers either on the fly through product knowledge or by performing research and following up with answers.

A sales presentation or conversation is the time to have a back-and-forth conversation between the sales associate and the prospective buyer or client. This is the time for an open dialogue and presentation of the features and benefits. The best sales presentation ends with a purchase. At least prior to the purchase decision, the presentation comes to an end with a closing question or offer to the consumer to make a purchase.

What happens then when the customer says "NO"? Is the dialogue still open? Can the salesperson come back with more benefits or a greater needs presentation? Is the sale over? Does the salesperson have the consumer's permission to continue?

The customer said "NO." What happens now? Novice salespersons will take "NO" and move on. Remember that old saying: it takes ten "NOs" to get to "YES." That is a 9 percent closing ratio. I do not have enough leads to take "NO" ten times and walk away. I sure would not like facing all those people over and over and taking "NO" for an answer that many times.

The Art of PASS - FAIL

Sales experts will suggest that the sale begins at "NO." Agreed.

The big question is: how does a salesperson go back to the pitch from "NO"?

Some so-called experts will tell you to respond by building more value. Others will suggest that you "overcome" the objection. Get back in there and hit the customer with more benefits. Do not take "NO" for an answer.

This just escalates the sales approach to a high-pressure sales pitch. The relationship that has been cultivated for the last five minutes, days, weeks, or years goes away. The salesperson runs the risk of ruining the relationship by adding what I call pressure to a "NO" situation. Jumping right back into the conversation when a "NO" is on the table is often frowned upon by the customer. Many salespeople decide to run away. Some consider that it is better to try again next time versus going back for the win.

L.E.A.D
Approach to Objection Handling

This book is about overcoming objections and customer management. The sale really does start at "NO." The reason you bought the book is to get a fresh look at objection handling and the best approach to retain the relationship while going back to battle and winning the sale. The whole idea is to pass more times than you fail. We can certainly have better odds of winning at our trade than just gambling at the casino.

I know many industries where high performers kick back and say 25 or 30 percent closing is a great ratio. Heck, one could get inducted into the Baseball Hall of Fame with a .300 batting average. This might get you millions in professional ball. In sales, 30 percent closing means we fail 70 percent of the time. You do the math.

The experts in Vegas say that blackjack will get you a win 44–48 percent of the time. If it takes ten "NO" responses to get a "YES," we are better off going to Las Vegas and learning how to play twenty-one. Forty-eight percent seems much better than one out of 11 or 9 percent.

$$10 \text{ "NO"} + 1 \text{ "YES"} = 11. \ 1/11 = 9\%$$
$$\text{VS}$$
$$\text{Blackjack } 48\%$$

For those odds, your employer is better off hanging out at the casino instead of spending money on you as the salesperson.

What if you failed 91 percent of the time with customer service? An argument could easily be made that you will be out of business very soon. If nine out of eleven hostile customers posted on social media, would you be able to cover up that message?

Our approach in the following pages will be the perfect approach for your customers, clients, and especially for your nightmare—aggressive customers. When handled correctly, these people will become your biggest ambassadors.

I want your company to take a chance on you and your ability to learn a simple approach. This approach is called LEAD. When you master the steps in this approach,

- *your sales will go up.*
- *your closing ratio will go up.*
- *your customer relationships will thrive.*
- *your personal relationships will improve.*
- *your life will change.*

LEAD is a proven model that I have used in training for over fifteen years. It has evolved into a recognized standard used in high-level sales and customer management nationwide and even worldwide. The LEAD approach works for both sales objections and customer management. In our first section, we will focus on overcoming objections with some references to customer handling. The latter part of this book will develop LEAD as a customer management tool.

Remember, LEAD is an acronym that stands for Listen, Empathize, Ask Questions, and Determine a Solution. The words are each a very distinct step in the process of objection handling. Notice I used the word process. Objection handling is a process. It is a learned skill. In fact, this process is a lifelong learned skill, which, when implemented, will change your life. The book is meant to be read in a short amount of time. The reader can certainly implement these tactics immediately. The reader will have immediate improved results. However, to become a master, the reader must practice this concept over and over at all opportunities.

John Maxwell, an internationally recognized leadership expert, suggests one must perform a task six thousand times to become an expert. Use that as a baseline. If you want to become an expert at sales, I suggest you get out there and make sales. If you suck at sales, you might want to learn this new approach. If you often get objections, do not blame the approach; look inside and find a better way. LEAD is a great approach to your sales objection. LEAD will work, and it will change your life. If you are good at sales and want to become better, LEAD can do that for you as well.

L = Listen
E = Empathize
A = Ask Questions
D = Determine a Solution

Listen - You have two ears and one mouth. That means you have to *listen* twice as much as you speak. The purpose of listening is to HEAR the customer. Hear the voice of the customer and the true objection. Listen to what the customer is saying. They are generally telling you exactly what they need to make the purchase.

The first part is the HEARING of the customer's words. Listen to hear and have the customer be heard. Once you believe you have truly heard the customer, then you must restate the words out loud back to the customer. It is important that the customer knows you heard them and their concern.

The goal is to acknowledge the customer. Everyone wants to be acknowledged. Everyone wants to be heard. Call it ego, but it is practically in our DNA. Look at me! The Facebook "like" button is the customer's ego. See me. Hear me. Acknowledge me. It is a social construct now. Social media is my ego, and I need you to feed it.

OK. If that is the case, then do it. Feed your customer's need to be heard and restate the objection or concern right back to them. You can simply repeat every part of the objection word for word. That works and is very formal.

The Art of PASS - FAIL

It is even more effective to summarize the objection and restate it back in a shorter phrase or in phrases. Listen to the whole objection and rephrase it back to the customer. In rephrasing, it is important to capture the essence of the objection. This can become tricky in translation. Be cautious when rephrasing. It is best to completely restate.

The expert salesperson can also do what is called mirroring and simply restate the last few words of the customer's objection. As the salesperson masters the concept, it is easier to mirror the customer. Formally, I teach the long version to learn the approach. I call it internalizing the approach. Internalizing is when we do not even have to think about it. It just happens naturally.

Until it becomes a habit or very natural, it is important to use a more formal approach. Listen to the customer's words and restate them back to the customer exactly as you heard them. This will ensure that the customer knows that you heard their words and they have been acknowledged.

As we peel back objections, I will share one simple phrase in the following pages for this step to ensure the customer has been acknowledged (HEARD).

Empathize - Empathy is the act of understanding or demonstrating that you share an understanding of the customer's situation. Volumes have been written on empathy, but I will attempt to simplify its definition. Empathy is the act of putting yourself in the customer's shoes.

The purpose of empathy is to demonstrate to the customer the similarity between you and the customer. Empathy is a way for you to position yourself as the advocate for the customer. Demonstrating empathy with your words, body language, or tone of voice is a way of aligning yourself with the customer. The goal is to gain the customer's acceptance of you as their activist. You are the one and only person who understands their needs, and you have the perfect solution. You have the most practical solution that fits their requirements. The act of aligning yourself with the customer sets you up to finally re-engage and present the solution in a new way.

Empathy can be a learned skill. Some individuals have more natural talent to demonstrate this skill than others. The more you can learn and practice empathy, the better position you will be in to overcome objections. The better you overcome objections, the more sales you will close and the more money you will make. This

The Art of PASS - FAIL

can be life-changing for the best, or at least for the ones who want to be the best.

These steps are presented in a logical order for the customer to respond best. It is fundamental to the success of the process that they are followed in order. It is also important to become a master of these steps. Anyone can be an order taker. The real skill, ability, or talent comes when we master this approach.

The purpose of this book is to take this massive idea of objection handling and give you a simple step-by-step approach to removing the objection. The approach of listening and empathizing is to make your customer a partner and solve the problem together. I will share one very simple phrase as this step progresses in the book that will allow others to see you as their equal or as having the same experience.

ASK Questions - The reason we ask questions is threefold. The first reason to ask questions is to gain permission to present a solution. The customer says "NO," and the presentation is over. Ask for permission to find out more details on the negative response. The next reason is for us, the salesperson, to clarify in our own minds the objection. We ask questions to be sure that we have a clear path to a solution. Once we are clear about the objection, we use questions to guide the customer to the best solution. Imagine the solution in your brain. Once you have a solution in mind, ask the customer what they think of your resolution in the form of a question.

The purpose of the questions is to promote a defense-free solution. First, gain the approval of the customer to continue. Remember, the client took time out to hear your solution to their problem. They have their needs. Your first attempt did not quite convince them. They still have a problem. Ask permission politely to suggest another solution. (Details to follow). Ask clarifying questions to develop a plan of action in your brain and then follow up with questions to guide the customer to the best solution—your product or service.

Determine the Solution - The last and final step is easy. Once the customer has approved the best solution, agree to the sale. You and your customer will agree on the best path and move forward in your relationship with the sale behind you.

Keys to Communication

This entire book is dedicated to developing better communication tools for the customer service representative or sales professional. These tools can be translated into any occupation or lifestyle. The LEAD method we are ultimately going to discuss in the following chapters will change your life—if you master the approach.

I have dedicated my life to making communication between sales and customer service professionals and their customers easy. As a lifelong researcher and student of people, I come across countless professors, trainers, and well-intentioned idiots trying to baffle you with their knowledge. Most take a simple topic and make it complicated. So many try to show how complicated a topic is so they will seem smarter or more important because they know these college-level or three-syllable words.

My philosophy is to make the ideas simple for everyone. My viewpoint is that if it is easy for the professional sales and customer service person, it is easy for the customer as well. Gee, what a great idea. The more useful the content, the more adaptable and more accepted it will become. Simple is the KEY. Most have heard of the KISS concept. Keep It Simple, Stupid. That's it. I want to discuss a simple topic to reinforce the concepts you know, such as words, tone of voice, and body language.

The book is not a guide to read others but a way to influence our personal style and presentation to the ultimate end user: the hostile customer, nuisance, or potential buyer of our product and service.

In my previous book, *Master of the Waiting Room*, I gave numerous examples of how the words we use influence our presentations. Now, I am going to expand upon this by sharing simple ideas, such as how the tone of voice and body language affect current customers and potential buyers.

There are three important types of communication:

- **Verbal**
- **Tone of voice**
- **Body language**

Verbal communication is obviously the words we use. In selecting the best words, and dare I say the least number of words, we can have a high impact on our presentation performance. Most people realize how important proper words are in the presentation. The truth is that words only communicate 7 percent of the message to the recipient.

Imagine that 93 percent of the message is lost with only words. Picture a text message that you received from a friend or colleague. Have you ever misinterpreted a message? We see the message and imagine the tone of the sender. That imagination is often wrong. Some even use all capital letters or emojis to convey tone. These are great illustrations of how important words are to the receiver and how important it is to not only choose the right message but say it in the right way.

The tone of our voice can be viewed as the way we speak our words. One could look at the tone of voice as our personality. Tone can take on many different effects. The tone of voice communicates an additional 38 percent of the message to the recipient. Great communicators rely on their tone to convey the message with emotion. We will discuss five types of tone of voice further in the chapter.

Body language is known as non-verbal communication. Body language is how we carry ourselves in a conversation. It is key to understand that 55 percent of the message is conveyed through body language. Great communicators also use their facial and body expressions to convey and transfer information. We will discuss five simple types of body language further in the chapter.

Communication Characteristics

Throughout the communication process, speakers, salespersons, and other customer professionals rely on three tools to ensure proper communication.

- ***Attention***
- ***Attitude***
- ***Adjustments***

Each of these characteristics is equally significant in the communication process. To begin with, the speaker must pay attention to the recipient. The customer must feel as if they are the most important person in the entire process. The speaker can demonstrate how they are paying attention by listening, asking questions, changing their tone of voice, nodding or shaking their head, and using other types of body language to show interest. This shows the listener that the speaker cares about the customer. It can convey the importance of the situation. Paying attention can improve customer relations and the ever-important social media response.

Next is the speaker's attitude. The speaker must demonstrate the proper attitude toward the customer, buyer, and topic. The speaker can express their passion and interest in the subject with the proper attitude. All types of communication are utilized to show the best attitude.

Using powerful, high-impact words to describe the scenario while smiling or confidently displaying the speaker's knowledge and experience indicates the proper outlook. The proper attitude reveals how interested the speaker is in the buyer or consumer.

Finally, the speaker must be willing to adjust and be open-minded. Generally, the one-size-fits-all approach to anything can fail. The speaker or professional needs to make course corrections and be willing to add or subtract tactically to drive the communication process.

Revealing one's willingness to adjust and be flexible certainly shows great communication skills. This is central to the sales and defusing process. The best speakers will utilize all the characteristics and personality traits to let the recipient know that they are valued and appreciated. This goes a long way toward the process of customer management. The best speakers will display all of these throughout the entire process. This comes with a mastery of communication and process.

Words have Meaning

The words we use have an impact on the customer's impression and their interpretation of said words. It is important to focus on high-impact words in our presentation versus overusing or trying to explain a concept. Many people just want us to get to the point.

In our presentations, it is important to use words such as the following:

- ***Required*** Versus ***Recommended***
- ***Necessary*** Versus ***Overdue***
- ***Important*** Versus ***Should***
- ***Pass – Fail*** Versus ***Good – Bad***
- ***Asking*** Versus ***Telling***

This is an instant-gratification world. People are looking for answers and not excuses. Most want to know facts versus opinion, as well as wanting to be led or asked versus being told. Today, people are not looking to be sold. They may want to buy things. However, most polled are not looking for a sales pitch. Make your case, and allow the customer to freely give you their money. Selling causes consumers to wall up and look for reasons to leave you. The fewer words spoken make the ones utilized more powerful. The phrase *less is more* speaks volumes. Make a pitch with simple, high-impact words. This will save future discussions and questions from the potential buyer.

Required Versus Recommend

To the customer, the word "recommend" means an opinion. Salespeople make recommendations, and in translation, it sounds like your personal view, not the facts. A recommendation is a sales pitch, and everyone who hears that word knows you are selling.

The Art of PASS - FAIL

For example,

- A. I recommend this TV. It has all the options you are looking for in a television. (*I want to sell you this TV as it pays me the highest commission.*)
- B. To meet all your requirements, this television fits perfectly. (The facts are ____. *Notice how a need was created by adding the word requirement into the presentation.*)

B = Facts, Requirement or Need. (Need + Value = Sale). The customer is at your electronics store. They see the value in you, and a need is created. A sale is made.

Necessary Versus Overdue

For example,

- A. This cable bill is overdue. *(My cable is still working, so why do I need to pay for it?)*
- B. It is necessary to pay the cable bill to continue service. *(Necessity creates a need. The customer will realize the service is about to be shut off.)*

B = Fact, Necessary or Need. The customer's mind sees the necessity of paying the bill.

Important Versus Should

A. You should get your teeth cleaned today. *(Stop telling me what to do. The word should is a command. People do* not *like to be told what to do.)*
B. It is important to have a teeth cleaning annually. *(Share how things are important and allow the customer to make a decision.)*

B = Fact, Important or Need. The customer will hear important things and not feel pushed.

Pass – Fail Versus Good – Bad

A. Those items look really good. Good is your opinion.
B. This item looks bad. Bad is your opinion.
C. There are items that pass inspection. Pass is a fact. There are items that fail inspection. Failure is a fact.

The Art of PASS - FAIL

B = Facts, Requirement or Need. Customers tend to purchase items that are needed. Fail shows an urgent need. I must buy it NOW. When items fail, or we fail at something, we must take immediate action.

Asking versus Telling

- A. Telling is adversarial. When most people are told what to do, human nature takes over, and resistance happens. They may feel backed into a corner and end the presentation or possibly escalate into hostility.
- B. It is polite and professional to ask a consumer a question. Asking questions allows the customer to feel as if they are in control. The customer will feel as if they can stop the presentation at any time.

B = Professionals ask questions to keep customers in control.

When we use soft, vague words (recommend, due, good, and bad), customers think we are just jabbering with our opinions. Many times, we are not granted expert status just because we are sales or service people. When we assume this expert status, it can backfire. Choosing the highest impact word at the right time for our presentation can ultimately save us time, get to the point faster, and help defuse the potentially hostile environment in front of us.

Notice how just a few words chosen at the right time can give the professional a tactical advantage in war. And yes, I said it again, this is a war for your company dollar and your paycheck. I fight for my money. If having a higher income, sales recognition, and a better lifestyle is important, choosing the right words at the right time can have a huge impact on your life.

Tone of Voice

Perform an internet search on tone of voice, and you may see thousands of types of tones. They can range from soft to operatic tones. Sounds complicated. Quite frankly, in a sales presentation, objection approach, or defusing a hostile customer, just having a few simple tools in your toolbox will serve you well.

Our material focuses the salesperson on our internal presentation. Other authors will share advice on how to read others and what all this gibberish means. I want to keep the focus on you and how you present yourself. Everyone has a unique set of skills. This depends on our life, work experience, and our position, whether entry-level or expert. There is a time and place to study others. I want to stay focused internally. As a customer service professional, I can only control my actions and persuade others based on my ability.

Let's say we examine five different types of tone of voice. I propose we examine our normal tone plus a range of two up and two down from normal. As the book progresses, you can fill in the blanks on which tone is appropriate at which time. You do not need me for that. This is a great refresher or reminder to utilize this tool that will enhance your presentation by 38 percent.

Confident + 2 Firm or Stern
Smiling + 1 Big Grin Voice
Normal = Everyday Voice
Soft – 1 Easygoing or Quiet Voice
Scared – 2 Quivering Nervous Voice

Those five types of tones can be seen as very simple voice expressions. As you review each of the word tones, imagine yourself having conversations with a potential buyer or hostile person. I encourage you to take a moment to decide which tone you will choose when engaging a customer. Read each tone as it is expressed on the page.

The Normal Tone - This is our everyday tone. Hey, I am just hanging out with friends, family, and colleagues. There is nothing special. It is just me and my words. Hopefully, you find this a natural way to speak. Nice and casual. I am not speaking fast or slow, just cruising along talking to a friend. NORMAL or NATURAL

Say this in a normal or natural tone.

> "We have dinner reservations at 6:00 p.m. this evening."

The Smiling Tone - Imagine something special in your life. Imagine a happy moment and create a real smile on your face. It shows. As you begin to follow the words on the page, smile and keep reading. Perform the same exercise as above and smile widely.

Exaggerate your smile for this statement.

> "We have dinner reservations at 6:00 p.m. this evening."

How did that sound to you? Did it make you happy? Would a customer notice a different way about you? Can the customer be influenced or persuaded by your smiling voice?

The Confident Tone - You are the foremost expert in your field with more experience in all areas. You are sure your product can fill the needs of the customer in front of you. In the next exercise, imagine you just acquired dinner reservations at the most popular restaurant in town.

Now you are about to tell your favorite person about your success in your most assured voice.

> "We have dinner reservations at 6:00 p.m. this evening."

WOW. Really? How did that confident tone change your statement? Can a family member, friend, or colleague be influenced by your assured tone?

The Soft Tone - Lower your voice a small amount. This is not a whisper, but your normal tone just taken down a little bit. Often, we do this to defuse someone who is yelling or using a stern, raised voice. This can have the perfect effect on an individual. It allows them to feel empowered. It also shows that you are not pushing back against them and are willing to hear what they are saying. You are relinquishing your power to allow them to have control.

Now tell your significant other, who is upset and angry, that you care about them while repeating the following phrase.

> "We have dinner reservations at 6:00 p.m. this evening."

Did that help defuse the yelling? Thank you for listening and taking care of this important item.

The Scared Tone - This tone shows our lack of confidence in the product or price. Often, new salespersons or customer service professionals are unsure of the outcome and possibly quiver at the thought of the high price, lack of availability, or some other reason. The scared tone often results in poor sales and unhappy results.

Imagine you forgot to make reservations for an important family event. The only time available is certainly not going to make everyone happy.

> *"Ummm . . . well . . . uh . . . we have dinner reservations at 6:00 p.m. this evening."*

Notice how your upper lip quivers and shakes as you deliver the message.

Body Language

The last type of communication is body language. Body language is non-verbal, yet it is the most powerful aspect of the entire process. The text here is designed for the reader to look inside and examine their body-language style and presentation approach. It is more central to know who you are than to try to read another's complex body language. Learning to read others is much more intricate. If we speakers work to make our body language the best, then we can convey a more professional and customer-friendly approach to the entire scenario in front of us. People in glass houses should not throw stones. Start with you and ensure your words have an impact. Decide on your tone, and illustrate your commitment with great posture, openness, and passion.

I am going to focus again on five simple body language styles:

> ***Open Arms + 2 Welcoming***
> ***Sitting or Standing Tall + 1 Confident***
> ***Normal - Everyday Posture***
> ***Hunched Over - 1 Bored***
> ***Crossed Arms - 2 Closed Off***

Body language is the most important way to communicate with your recipient. As noted earlier, 55 percent of the message is communicated through our posture. Body language carries the message that our words leave behind. My words may say "YES;" however, my face could say "NO." My head nodding up and down while asking a question shows my confidence in the discussion. Crossing my arms may have the opposite effect. This could signal I am done and not willing to budge.

Normal Posture

This is how we relax and sit to work or play. We are casual and comfortable. Read the following sentence aloud with your casual body posture, most likely just as you are sitting now.

The Art of PASS - FAIL

My name is (Insert Your Name). I am here to help you.

That was easy. Hey, my name is Steve Shaw. Relaxed and comfortable.

Sitting or Standing Tall Posture

Now sit or stand up tall in your seat or office. Feel the confidence come over you. Take a big deep breath of fresh air and state the same line.

My name is (Insert Your Name). I am here to help you.

That was confident. The customer appreciates your willingness to work together to resolve their situation. Great job on that confidence factor.

Open Arms Posture

This time, as you read this line, stretch out your arms, take that deep breath and fill your heart with kindness. It naturally leads to a smile, and you say,

Welcome! My name is (Insert Your Name). I am here to help you.

Doesn't that feel amazing? Imagine your customer or buyer feeling the exuberance of welcoming them into your family. Imagine the walls crumbling as a distressed person arrives at your counter. The open arms approach gives the feeling of acceptance.

<u>Hunched Over Posture</u>

Elbows on the table, hands on your chin, shoulders hunched into that slouch. Feelings of boredom, anxiety, and a longing to end this misery come over you. Say the same statement hunched over.

My name is (Insert Your Name). I am here to help you.

Gee, thanks. I am looking for someone else who wants to help me. Your negativity is shining through far beyond your words of helpfulness. Please find another person who can help me.

Crossed Arms Posture

You are sitting back in your chair or standing up, possibly leaning against the wall or a post. Your arms are crossed. This could lead to a stern look or even a frown. Some may wonder about the tough day you are presenting. Most avoid you. Imagine that you are in this position, and a guest walks to your podium as you state,

> **My name is (Insert Your Name). I am here to help you.**

This posture says, "Go Away. I am deep in thought. I have so many problems, and now you are the next issue on my list. I am closed off. I dislike the world right now."

Yikes. We cannot end a chapter with the anxiety of being cross-armed and hunched over. Go back and recall that smiling tone of voice, and open your arms and heart wide, take that big deep breath of pure self-confidence, grin from ear to ear, and say,

> **I love my job. I am amazing and powerful. The world is waiting for me to present positive change!**

With only a few written words about language, we can make a huge difference in our lives. Imagine the phone calls, text messages, and emails that we are using as a medium of delivery. Notice how each and every word impacts the narrative. Now focus on your tone as you write or speak. Adjust your body into a positive position and develop the best script to deliver your message.

The words we use, the personality in the delivery, and our body posture can certainly affect our conversations. They can be affected by our attitude, attention, and willingness to adapt. Make a conscious effort to shift your energy toward the communication before a word is spoken. Watch the improved results.

Step-By-Step - Listen

Let's examine each step further and in-depth. It is important to recognize the pitfalls of objection handling. Sometimes, based on our experience, we use words that counter the message we are trying desperately to convey. Often because of culture or even observation of others, we use simple words that repel others when we are trying to connect. Every word and action we take conveys a message to the recipient. This message can be positive or negative, which can influence or impair the sale. As we discussed earlier, words have meaning.

The customer has politely said, "NO, thank you." In their mind, the sales presentation has come to an end. The next few words that you speak will determine the success or failure of your entire presentation. The next few words and actions determine if you are going to make that bonus you are counting on to pay for that exotic vacation. The next words determine your passing or failing grade. The next words may have an impact on your life. When "NO" happens, each individual goes through a process and makes a decision based on all the factors surrounding the entire scenario. It all boils down to a decision. Do I pack up my wares and retreat for another chance? Or do I saddle up for the ride of a lifetime? The ride of your life starts when you make the decision to OVERCOME THE OBJECTION.

If you choose to take this step into a brave new world, I salute you for your determination. Anyone can take an order. Anyone can fill an order. Not everyone can take "NO" for an answer. I certainly try to minimize the "NO" response from a customer. However, when that bell rings, I answer that call.

> Nearly fifteen years ago, I started my training company. Yes, I am an experienced car dealership professional. I have had the opportunity to manage the biggest auto groups in the country. My experience and knowledge led me to start

Steve Shaw Training. However, I did not have experience selling myself to prospective new car dealerships. My story might be slightly exaggerated as my memory caters to how good I am. We all exaggerate the truth when it serves us well. However, I do remember how broke I was about one year into my new life as a trainer-consultant. When I say broke, I mean flat broke, like "Where is the gas money coming from next?" broke. I needed to start exploring job openings again.

I had been courting a new car dealership in Tampa, Florida, for a few weeks on the introduction by a now good friend and close colleague. The time had come to stop the pleasantries and the arm sniffing and ASK for the JOB! *Sir (Name Redacted), it sounds like we are on the same page. I have a very good understanding of your situation, and Steve Shaw Training can help you improve your business. How about we make a plan and get this project going in your dealership? I have an availability opening in two weeks.*

The Art of PASS - FAIL

We discussed the necessary investment, and I was ready to start on my improvement plan.

Well, Steve, I do agree we could work well together, he stated. *However, as we discussed earlier, I am unsatisfied with the current management, and I think a change is in order before we start. I want to have the right candidate in place, you know. I hate to spend all this money with you just to have some new person want to try a different approach.*

My mind went in so many directions in a split second. The thoughts ranged from *F*@K ME* to *F*@K HIM* to *Now what?* and every thought in between. At the same time, I had to dig deep into my soul and decide on my future. How do I pay the bills? How do I live my best life? How do I face my family with a failed business? What do I do right now at this moment? All these thoughts powered through my brain in what may have seemed like a long weekend retreat in the Peruvian jungle lounging around drinking ayahuasca and tripping around the universe. I'll save that story for another book. I felt like I had been hit over the head, and a gong rang out in my mind, bringing me back to reality.

SHAW . . . Wake Up, BRO! You are a sales trainer. You have more knowledge and expertise than any other human being. You possess a Bachelor of Science in Automotive Service Technology, a Master's Degree in Business Administration, and a Doctorate in Human Behavior and Organizational Leadership. This is your life. Do something!! Now!! Now!!

Remember I stated that the next words out of your mouth can change your life? Mine certainly did.

Me: Sir, if I hear you correctly, you are interested in working together. (*YES*, came a word of response out of nowhere.) *What I heard is that you are unsatisfied with your manager and really do* not *want to spend money now and just end up wasting it with a new guy. Is that correct?*

The Art of PASS - FAIL

Him: YEP. You know how new managers are; they all want to do it their way.

Me: So, how did I do? I just acknowledged the dealer's principal issue. Wait a minute, that was textbook acknowledgment. I went on to say, (to conclude the story) *If I were in your shoes, I would probably feel the same way. I sure hate for anyone to waste money. May I ask you a question?* He agreed. *What would you think about hiring me as your outside consultant? I can take care of hiring and firing for you. We together can find a new manager who shares your philosophy, and soon you will have everything that you want out of your team.*

Him: You know, Steve, that sounds great. I wanted to take a vacation and having you here to guide the new guy would be great. What date can you start?

Fifteen years later, my life has changed for the better!

There is something deep down inside us that is driving

our decision to be better salespersons and customer service professionals. If you are reading this book, you have made the commitment to improve yourself. I shared a story of how I took my training and applied it to my work. I had success when the client said, "No thanks." I am going to share the strategy step-by-step.

Step One

Listen to your customer - Listen to hear what the customer is saying to you. Pay attention to the words. Listen to clearly understand the objection or complaint. Overcoming objections and defusing a hostile situation require the exact same approach. Your customer or nuisance has a situation that requires your immediate attention. Your customer or nuisance needs to be HEARD. Your job is to listen to hear, hear the reason and acknowledge the person with the concern. Step one is to listen and restate or acknowledge the person with whom you are interacting.

We are all ego-driven individuals. From the moment we make our first sounds as infants, we are driven by our ego. The first sounds we make, from ga-ga goo-goo to those times we crawl and finally that first step of walking, we crave attention from our parents or loved ones. "Look at me," we say. Pay attention to me is what we crave. As we grow, it is simple human nature to seek out attention. Imagine back as a child the times we sought out and received attention. The parent smiled and gave props to the youngster for even the simplest of tasks. The parent acknowledges the accomplishment. Our hearts and ego grow with the recognition of triumph.

Today's culture of social media is similar. Facebook, Twitter, and the like are all media for attention. People are seeking and receiving attention. Social media now has a term for people with lots of followers called influencers. Social media influencers crave attention, recognition, and acknowledgment. Some are monetarily rewarded for being popular. Modern society places value on the recognition of everything. Your customer or nuisance is one of those people who want and crave attention. They may or may not realize it at that moment. If you want a financial reward for your efforts, then give them what they want—acknowledgment.

In the auto industry, we have a saying that if a customer puts a $3 badge (which is a sticker) on a $30,000 vehicle, it must be important to that customer. It says, "Look at me. I love the St. Louis Cardinals." "My child is an honor student" is another badge of honor or recognition. Cars with bumper stickers, fancy paint jobs, rims and wheels, and raised or lowered suspension litter the streets and highways. All of this is done for one reason—ego or recognition. "Look at me! Acknowledge me! My Jeep Wrangler is orange, for heaven's sake. Look at me!"

Acknowledgment is the key to moving forward in the process. This step starts by recognizing the words being said and repeating them back to the customer. Over time, the professional will develop their own style of persuasion. Your words may evolve as you internalize the process. That is positive. That demonstrates your adoption of the method.

The formal approach is to restate exactly the words from the customer who declined or the nuisance customer. This lets the speaker know they have BEEN HEARD. When the nuisance suddenly realizes that they have been heard, it is as if the wind is being released from the sail. The situation is being defused right in front of your eyes. The prospective customer who declined the sale realizes that they have been heard, and then they begin to let down their guard. They decided to say "NO" to you, and a wall came up. "NO!" The process is ending. "STOP!" When the customer's brain hears the same words coming from you, the professional salesperson, a connection is made between both parties. The wall starts to lower. Perfect! That is exactly what is supposed to happen. The connection is made, and there is a release of invisible tension between everyone. I, potential customer or nuisance, have been HEARD.

Think back to a time when you went to a restaurant. The server comes out, greets you at the table, and you exchange pleasantries. The server, without notes, advises you of the chef's specials, and now your party begins to order. The server has no pen or paper and simply nods as the party orders and continuously changes the order. The server completes the table order and heads back to the kitchen. Is the table impressed or nervous?

The evidence shows that most patrons are nervous about their orders. Some argue that it's cool to memorize, some say it is about control, and some say it is a bonding experience. Most restaurant patrons say they just want their order correct. Take out a pen and write down my order! Restate my order back to me. I came to the restaurant to enjoy the meal that I ordered, not to worry about the mess that might be made with my dinner. The purpose is to acknowledge the order and then ensure the kitchen prepares it correctly.

This scenario sounds exactly like the potential customer situation. Look at "NO" as the real beginning of the sale. The salesperson made a presentation based upon their interpretation of the needs, wants or desires of the potential buyer.

The presentation ends. The potential buyer says, "NO, thank you," and cites a particular reason. Where is the salesperson now? If you pack up and prepare to leave, you just walked away from the biggest sale of your life. At this moment, the salesperson has been handed a gift. The gift is the answer, the way, the solution, the one item keeping the potential buyer from actually opening the corporate wallet and keeping you from a big fat commission check. This is exactly where the salesperson wants to be sitting. Can you picture sitting in front of the biggest client and knowing exactly what you must do to sell a job? Wow, I can count the dollar signs right now. I have a pool in mind for the backyard.

No = A Gift

Wait, you have a nuisance in front of you that is about to drop a bomb and then serve up the ultimate solution or reason for their anger. That sounds like the perfect scenario. The job of the customer service professional just got that much easier. My stress level is about to lower immensely. I may even go home early tonight.

The Art of PASS - FAIL

You were just given the road map to the minefield. Make no mistake about it. There are bombs that can easily go off. The key is to acknowledge or restate the objection without escalating to the nuisance or having the potential buyer feel pressure. There are loaded mines in this war, remember? I will give you the million-dollar phrase in a moment. First, we need to discuss two words to avoid. The BOMBs.

What **not** *to say*

Never say "I UNDERSTAND!"

"I UNDERSTAND" is a time bomb just waiting to blow. I know you want to use that word. That dreaded U word. Don't do it! Your guts, wallet, and job prospects will be spread across the board room, and HR might be notified. The word "understand" is to be avoided at all costs. The reason is that YOU cannot tell ME that YOU understand ME or MY situation. For one reason, empathy is the second step, and you are trying to demonstrate empathy prior to acknowledging the situation. BOOM! It is impossible for you to convey the message at this moment that you UNDERSTAND ME! As my mentor, Jim Floodman, would say, "Hear me now and believe me later." I will dive into the U word in more detail later. The second reason and, more importantly, the first step is acknowledgment. The prospective customer or nuisance needs to be HEARD, not understood.

What else should you avoid saying? "I am SORRY." "Sorry" is the second time bomb ready to blow. Just because I did not buy from you, you are "sorry." Just because I am upset, you say "sorry." Saying "sorry" is not appropriate in this scenario. I will discuss the proper time to offer a sincere apology. The word "sorry" has almost no meaning on its own. A customer can interpret the phrase "I'm sorry" as slang or a casual phrase meaning "Yeah, Yeah, I hear you. Now let's move on. Let's sweep it under the rug and move on. Nothing to see here; let's move on." "Sorry" has taken on a flippant implication. Picture how many times today, this week, or this month someone has said "SORRY" to you.

Leroy Jethro Gibbs of the Hit series NCIS will tell you rule #6 is "Never say you're sorry: it's a sign of weakness.

Bumped into you in the hallway. "Sorry."
Cut you off mid-sentence. "Sorry."
"Sorry" your phone quit working. "Sorry."

"Sorry," "sorry," "sorry." It means nothing, especially in this context.

People randomly say "oops, sorry" to be polite. The proper term is "excuse me." "Sorry" is now casual slang for "excuse me."

Imagine when a nuisance offers the problem, and someone casually says, "Well, excuse me!" If you are old enough, refer to the old Steve Martin comedy bit on YouTube. "WELLLL EXCUUUUSSSE ME!"

Or

The potential buyer says thanks for the presentation; however, the product does not have the necessary features like auto stop as we require. The salesperson says, "Well, excuse me! I guess I wasted my time here!"

BOOM!

In our previous chapter, we talked about how words mean things. Words have meaning, some positive and some negative. Both words "sorry" and "understand" have a negative meaning in this scenario. My suggestion is to avoid using these two words. It will save you lots of unnecessary dancing in the minefield.

The best way to approach a potential buyer or nuisance is to master this one phrase. "If I hear you correctly, (restate the objection exactly as the buyer stated)." Notice the proper phrase in this step. Listen to the issue and restate back to the customer exactly as they said it to you.

If I hear you correctly

(FILL IN THE BLANK - RESTATE THE OBJECTION)

" _____ "

Master this phrase, and you will be waltzing carefreely through the minefield with a road map on the way to empathy.

Review the list of objections and learn to master

Step one: **Listen and Restate**.

The Art of PASS - FAIL

- It costs too much.
- Not enough time.
- I need to talk to my spouse about a major purchase.
- This product does not have the features I am looking for.
- I found the same item cheaper somewhere else.

Now review each item with our acknowledgment phrase.

If I hear you correctly, the item costs too much?
If I hear you correctly, you do not have enough time?
If I hear you correctly, you need to talk to your spouse about a major purchase?
If I hear you correctly, the product does not have the features you are looking for?
If I hear you correctly, you found the same item cheaper elsewhere?

Some professionals may insert the word "feel." "If I hear you correctly, *you feel* the item costs too much?" That works as well. Do not, however, interpret this to be the "feel, felt, found" technique. That was a popular objection technique from the past. Today, there are flaws in telling the customer what you found.

> ~~I understand you feel this way.~~
>
> ~~Once I felt the same way.~~
>
> ~~I found that doing this would fix it.~~

Notice how the potential customer's objection was acknowledged. The speaker said, "If I HEAR you," and now the customer has been HEARD. Simple.

Potential complaints

I was overcharged by $100 on my bill this month.

I was promised a deluxe suite for my stay with my family.

My meal was cold, and I am not paying.

Your salesperson said everything was covered, bumper to bumper.

The parts did not arrive on time, and it cost me an extra $50 for a taxi.

Review the list of nuisance complaints and begin to master step one by listening to and restating the concern.

The Art of PASS - FAIL

If I hear you correctly, you were overcharged by $100 on your bill this month?

If I hear you correctly, you were promised a deluxe suite for your stay with your family?

If I hear you correctly, your meal was cold, and you don't feel you should pay?

If I hear you correctly, the salesperson said everything was covered bumper to bumper?

If I hear you correctly, the parts did not arrive on time, and it cost you an extra $50 for a taxi?

Notice as well in the above scenarios how the nuisance's complaint was simply acknowledged.

If I hear you correctly,

(FILL IN THE BLANK - RESTATE THE CUSTOMER ISSUE)

_____?

When acting inquisitively, softening your tone, and using your tone, and using your body language, it becomes natural to ask, "If I hear you correctly_____. Is that right?

The goal is for the customer to say, "Yes, that is correct." Often, they will give you more details.

Notice in the example:

> *Customer Objection*
>
> *Customer: I cannot buy this television today. That just costs too much money.*
>
> *Salesperson: If I hear you correctly, you cannot buy this television today because it costs too much money? Is that correct?*
>
> *Customer: Yes, I remember reading online about the same TV costing a lot less money. I must remember where I read that.*
>
> *(The customer read somewhere about a lower price TV; that is new information). The salesperson is collecting all the data to formulate a solution. Remember, the customer is standing in front of you, so*

they must see value in your store to be there in the first place.

Nuisance Complaint

Nuisance: My meal was cold, and I am not *paying for any of our meals on the check.*

Manager: If I hear you correctly, your meal was cold, and you are not *paying for any of the meals on the check? Is that correct?*

Nuisance: Yes, exactly. Your server brought out my soup first, and it took another ten minutes for my family to get their dinner. Why should I have to pay for bad food?

Notice that the nuisance gave more details about the problem. I am not even suggesting that the meal is free to the nuisance; however, you are getting more information to help solve the issue. This is step one. ACKNOWLEDGE the nuisance's complaint. The nuisance is losing steam now. The complaint is on the table, and they have been heard.

Step One – *Listen to and restate* the customer's objection or complaint. Each step in the process takes you closer to the discussion of the solution. Customer management is a process. It is a lifelong learned skill. The approach may sound or appear to be a bit "clunky," and that is okay for now. The goal is that when you hear an objection or complaint, you begin to listen in order to repeat back to the person making the statement. When you use that acknowledgment phrase, it is a formal approach to the situation. Over time, as your skills improve, you may start summarizing or mirroring the words of the customer.

A summary statement may not be exactly word for word as stated to you. The customer may have told you a long story about what happened to them or possibly a lengthy statement about why they cannot buy from you today. You may want to summarize the customer's words and restate as best you can a short version of the story. I want to offer words of caution to be very clear with your summary and even ask them if your summary is correct.

If I hear you correctly, summarize the situation and repeat it out loud. Then say, *Did I catch everything you said accurately? Yes. Great. I want to make sure I completely recognize your concern.*

The Art of PASS - FAIL

You are looking for recognition from the customer that you have an accurate picture of the issue. This is exactly where you want to be in the process.

Expert customer managers will do what is called mirroring. This is where you just repeat the last few words that were said. This is a skillful approach that requires lots of practice.

*Customer: I can't afford to purchase this sound system today. I have been out of work for seven months, and man, **I am tapped out**.*

Salesperson: Tapped out?

Customer: I get paid for my new gig in a few weeks. I can come back then.

Notice the skill in the acknowledgment. The expert salesperson captured the essence of the objection—the customer being "tapped out."

Or

*Customer: I can't afford to purchase this sound system today. I have been out of work for **seven months**, and man, I am tapped out.*

Salesperson: Seven months?

Customer: I get paid for my new gig in a few weeks. I can come back then.

Another expert may have decided that seven months was the essence of the conversation. Therefore, practicing your craft is vital. Both salespersons' responses may be correct. It depends on the conversation and where the emphasis is placed by the customer.

Step-By-Step - Empathize

Empathy is the act of understanding. This understanding can be to demonstrate to your adversary that you are alike. Empathy is being able to demonstrate your awareness of others' thoughts, feelings, or situations. Empathy, in the simplest form, is the ability to relate to another person's situation. Empathy is the act of putting yourself in the customer's shoes. Empathy is displayed through words, body language, and tone of voice.

According to Webster's dictionary, empathy is "the action of understanding, being aware of, being sensitive to, and vicariously experiencing the feelings, thoughts, and experience of another of either the past or present without having the feelings, thoughts, and experience fully communicated in an objectively explicit manner."

Human nature leads us to attempt to relate to others around us. Humans relate in life by sharing stories in conversation about similar situations. Often in conversation, one person tells a story, and the next tells a similar story to show that the two are the same. Imagine a first date where the prospective couple talks about life situations. Habitually, each continues the story and leads the other to the next layer in the conversation. As the date unfolds, depending on how alike the two determine they are to each other, a possible second date happens.

I can attest to many dinner conversations where a father started out discussing how difficult his day was, and then an offspring would talk about his challenges. Ultimately, bonding occurs. This type of scenario unfolds too many times to list in one chapter. That pair bonding, if only for a short time, is the feeling the salesperson or customer service professional is seeking. The speaker is hoping that the recipient notices the similarity and lowers their guard or lessens the hostility toward them.

It can be said that nuisance customers tend to be less hostile toward those who are similar or those they have feelings toward. In a friendship or relationship between known individuals or even colleagues, this bonding is a natural course. Sometimes the rapport is built immediately. People say, "We just clicked." In a sales transaction or a nuisance scenario, that is exactly what the speaker is trying to accomplish. By demonstrating empathy and making that immediate connection, the speaker is attempting to bypass the natural defenses of the nuisance or objecting client long enough to resolve the situation.

Speakers use visual, auditory, or kinesthetic words to connect with their audience. The science of Neuro-Linguistic Programming (NLP) is built upon one's ability to quickly connect with another. Corporate marketing campaigns and television and internet advertising are deeply rooted in the ability to quickly connect with the audience through NLP. Although I do have a mastery of this approach, I will leave the volumes of NLP science and rhetoric to Richard Bandler, the founder of NLP, and his followers. I am certain of his influence on my career and this writing.

As the second step of our LEAD process unfolds, it is vital to be aware that empathy and sympathy have a root similarity, but they are distinctly two different sensations.

The Art of PASS - FAIL

Sympathy

Sympathy in the art of customer service is the act of feeling "sorry" or even pity for another. I have sympathy or tenderness or concern or kindness toward someone or someone's situation. Pity may draw feelings of contempt toward someone or the situation.

The similarities between empathy and sympathy are sharing a feeling. You may have empathy toward my situation and relate without an emotional attachment. When you have sympathy, the emotional connection is stronger and generally in a sad or gentle way. Think of this simply as empathy is relating, and sympathy is feeling "sorry."

It is to be hoped that the salesperson leaves sympathy at the door during a sales transaction. If one cannot check their emotions, sales jobs may not be the best profession. Along with that, as one masters the concept of empathy sales, objection handling, and nuisance, negotiation becomes a satisfying trade.

Two Scenarios

A customer drives his new Ferrari into the dealership. He states how he accidentally *drove over a curb, and the entire exhaust system was ripped from the engine. The dealership informed him that the replacement cost was nearly $5000. This was a reasonable cost as the sticker price on the car was nearly $300,000. The customer is in shock; he breaks down and sobs. As the story unfolds, he states how he had just retired and spent his life savings on the car. He has no way of coming up with $5000 because he is on a fixed income.*

Sympathy Scenario – The dealership service person feels sorry for him and provides a deep discount or possibly a free exhaust system. Wrong! Even Ferrari dealerships must make a profit. The dealership would go broke if they provided sympathy service. Truthfully, owning a high-performance sports car is expensive. The man obviously overspent without considering any future needs for his luxury automobile.

Empathy Scenario – The dealership service person demonstrates empathy and relates to the owner. We have all been in situations where we did not have the extra funds for unexpected repairs. Correct. Now, as the two connect, they can work together to find an amicable solution.

Sympathy Example

A customer drives into a Ford Dealership with a Ford Focus. The technicians perform routine maintenance and notice a list of additional items that require immediate attention. The service person presents the items to the customer, and she breaks down and cries. She goes on to explain her situation as well as the drastic medical condition of her young daughter. The service person takes pity on this customer and takes up a collection among co-workers, along with a deep discount from the dealership, then pays the entire bill for the customer. GREAT. That was just an amazing scenario that everyone graciously contributed. No fanfare, just good people solving problems for a deserving woman.

Dos and Don't

Do

Demonstrate your ability to empathize with your customer. Demonstrate through your words, tone, and body language. The message you are attempting to convey is that you are just like them. This idea is to let them know that you are or have been in their shoes.

This is sometimes even an act or action. The best way of acting is to share a story. Share a quick scenario about how you have been through the same situation. Maybe your story is about a spouse, relative, friend, or another person who has had the same condition. By acting "as if," you are putting yourself in their shoes.

The message comes through by utilizing tone of voice and body language cues. Every scenario is different and requires skillful mastery and natural delivery. Practice your tone and body language with close friends and or practice partners until you are ready. Empathy is a learned skill for many. If you are one of the lucky ones to have a natural ability to relate, this step flows easily.

The Art of PASS - FAIL

Don't

Do not say you are sorry. The Urban Dictionary says that "I'm sorry" is a phrase carelessly thrown around by people who want to lessen their guilt. It does not convey that they care about the person who was hurt. It becomes a word for a quick relief that attempts to sweep the problem under the rug and move on! "Sorry" means I am not sorry. Let's be clear: saying "sorry" is not an apology. Saying "sorry," according to the Urban Dictionary, means you do not care. I encourage you to count the number of times people with low self-esteem say "sorry" to you each day.

Again, according to the Urban Dictionary, the purpose of an apology is to convey that the relationship is more important than my ego. Webster's will tell you that an apology is an expression of regret. The time to present a sincere apology is when one has regret about an action. A sincere apology may be an example: I regret my actions taken toward you. I will do my best not to do that in the future.

I apologize for not taking your feelings into account when did... I will do my best to be more considerate in the future.

Don't say "I understand." Remember, in the previous chapter, "I understand" is a phrase that says *I do not care. Let's move on!*

The best phrase to demonstrate empathy is as follows. "If I were in your shoes, I might feel the same way." This phrase exactly tells the nuisance or objector that you clearly understand what they are going through. This phrase conveys the precise message you are trying to deliver. Empathy is demonstrating that you feel the same way or putting yourself in their shoes. So, tell them that exactly! Simply say to the person in front of you, "If I were in your shoes, I might feel the same way." You can use this phrase as a stand-alone statement. Or you may use this as a bridge to a story that you would like to tell. For you lucky and talented empathetic people, add this to the beginning of your demonstration story and notice what happens. Notice how you are accepted as a partner.

If I were in your shoes. I might feel the same way!

*Customer: I can't afford to purchase this sound system today. I have been out of work for **seven months**, and man, I am tapped out.*

The Art of PASS - FAIL

Listen – Salesperson: Seven months?

Customer: Yeah, it has been a struggle to pay the bills around the house.

Empathize – Salesperson: If I were in your shoes, I might feel the same way. (Stand-alone statement)

*Customer: I can't afford to purchase this sound system today. I have been out of work for **seven months,** and man, I am tapped out.*

Listen – Salesperson: Seven months?

Customer: Yeah, it has been a struggle to pay the bills around the house.

Empathize – If I were in your shoes, I might feel the same way. (Bridge to additional empathy) Before this job, I was out of work for months myself.

Customer: Thanks for saying that.

The goal is to have the customer respond with a statement of "exactly" or "that's right."

Nuisance: My meal was cold, and I am not paying for any of our meals on the check.

Listen – Manager: If I hear you correctly, your meal was cold, and you are not-paying for any of the meals on the check? Is that correct?

Nuisance: Yes, exactly. Your server brought out my soup first, and it took another ten minutes for my family to get their dinner.

Empathize – Manager: If I were in your shoes, I might feel the exact same way as you. (stand-alone)

Nuisance: My meal was cold, and I am not paying for any of our meals on the check.

Listen – Manager: If I hear you correctly, your meal was cold, and you are not paying for any of the meals on the check? Is that correct?

Nuisance: Yes, exactly. Your server brought out my soup first, and it took another ten minutes for my family to get their dinner. Really bummed us out tonight.

Empathize – Manager: If I were in your shoes, I might feel the exact same way as you. (bridge-statement) I

The Art of PASS - FAIL

know how important my nights are with my family as well. Food really brings the family together.

Notice how the dissatisfied customer is losing steam. It becomes less likely that they will remain hostile because they realize they have been heard and you have aligned yourself with them. Imagine a balloon deflating as the air escapes or the beautiful sailboat gliding across the water, coming to a stop as the wind dies down and the boat comes to a rest. This is exactly what is happening to your nuisance customer. The emotions they are projecting are being released into thin air. You have successfully defused the nuisance and aligned yourself with them.

Picture the customer who said "No, thank you" and put up the wall to end the sales transaction. As you align yourself with them, that wall of "NO" is demolished; it falls, and the barrier between the two of you is gone. It is as if the two, who were once competitors, are now on the same side, staring at the problem together. You are in alignment with each other joining forces to solve the big objection.

This is exactly the place where you want to be right now. You now have been informed by your nuisance of the reason for their frustration. You have been given perfect instructions from your customer on what you need to provide to complete the sale. In fact, you are in a better position than even a few moments prior because you are in 100 percent alignment with your former adversary. You are just the person to solve the problem. You have just made yourself the tool with which the antagonist is going to achieve their needs.

BAM! How does that feel?

You are poised to win this challenge. You are now set up for success. Bask in that glory for a moment right here. Picture all the "NO, thank yous" you have been given—the lost opportunities. Picture those nuisance customers standing in front of you and your mind racing to find the proper words to respond. Imagine now, and going forward, they are a step on the path to victory. Victory in war to your big fat paycheck. Success in the path to smooth customer relations, and look at those amazing social media reviews. You are "The Man," and you completely turn any negative into a positive. I see a promotion in your future!

OH, NOW the fun part. Your expertise.

Step-By-Step - Ask Clarifying Questions

You are the problem solver. In the role of salesperson, one is expected to have expert product knowledge. The salesperson is also likely to have interpersonal skills, communication skills, as well as the ability to think on the fly and find solutions. The customer service professional may have additional and similar skills. The customer service professional is expected to know the company policy and procedures and have an arsenal of tools available in the case of upset customers. Each of these roles probably has certain avenues to make necessary adjustments as they see fit in each scenario.

The Art of PASS - FAIL

In our LEAD approach, first you must know your avenues of adjustment. What are the options that you can provide for a customer or potential client? At this point, I assume you know the possibilities that you can present in the event of an objection or a distressed customer.

The point of using the LEAD approach is NOT telling the customer the solution. LEAD allows the customer to come to their own conclusions with you. This is done by asking questions and guiding the person to the best solution. Guiding the customer to realize that you do have the best features and you do have the answer to their problem is a much better tactic than telling them. The point of chapter 2 is to create buyers.

We create buyers in the process of LEAD by asking questions—questions that guide the customer down the path to the solution. Remember: you and your client are in alignment. The nuisance is no longer furious. They are defused and ready to move forward. The "NO" is now open-minded, as you are a partner in the solution. This is the time to provide a solution in the form of a question. Yes, this sounds like Jeopardy. "Provide the answer in the form of a question," says Alex. But now I'm just dating myself.

The best way to get into the solution with your new partner is to ask permission to move forward. The goal is to continue down a path with your partner in full communion. The partner needs this as much as you. They have a problem that your widget will solve. They have a situation that they need resolved. You have established yourself as the provider of the solution in the last two steps. Do not blow it. Ask permission to move forward using this question.

May I ask you a question?

Wait, what? It's that simple? Yes!

May I ask you a question – *to resolve this issue further?* May I ask you a question – *so I can provide you with a solution to the objection?* That is what you are saying.

Naturally, your new partner is going to say "Yes," "Sure," or "OK!" You are now poised to bring this sale to a close or resolve the issue in front of you. Asking permission keeps the customer feeling as if they have the power or control in the process.

Once you become partners by listening twice as much, acknowledging the concern, and demonstrating empathy by aligning yourself with the customer, a simple question allows the process to move forward to the *Asking Questions* phase. Remember, we ask questions to guide the customer to the ultimate solution.

There are questions that help the salesperson. There are questions that help the customer service pro. There are other types of questions that range from simple conditional to closing styles as well. The goal of our book is to simplify the process. That does not mean this is a "one two three, and I am the expert." This means that by taking the approach of overcoming objections and mastering three simple phrases, you can position yourself as the one and only solution provider. You will be in the position of solving or resolving any outstanding issues in front of you and your new partner.

Solving problems and overcoming objections are advanced approaches. They do require a lifetime of practice and understanding. A key point to be aware of is that there are multiple dimensions to questions. Some questions require a yes or no answer. Some questions are open-ended. More importantly, there are questions that raise the level of importance and **move the conversation along faster to the solution.**

Four Types of Questions

I have categorized the questions into four categories. Even the most high-level question can be open-ended or a yes/no style. Salespersons or service professionals can ask open-ended or close-ended questions. Open-ended questions allow the customer to speak their thoughts. An example of an open-ended question is "What is important to you today?" The customer is forced to give a real answer about what is important to them. A close-ended question only requires a yes or no answer. An example would be "Is safety important to you?" The customer may say "No," and the salesperson is no further along in the conversation than before. It is important to ask open-ended questions to gain the insight needed.

We ask questions to provoke thought and to gain insight into a customer's thought process. In sales, the salesperson often does most of the talking. It is even more important to ask questions during the objection-handling phase. The salesperson must be able to ask these probing questions to get the proper result. Questioning can often be the hardest part of the sale. Many professionals feel uncomfortable probing. Remember, that's where empathy comes in. Once the salesperson has established the alignment with the customer, probing is a natural part of the process.

Silence or Pause

Very often, after a question comes, there is an awkward pause or silence from the customer. In advanced selling, it is important to become comfortable with the awkwardness. The customer is often formulating an answer to the question. WAIT, do not speak. A question was posed, and now it's time for an answer from the customer.

Experts will tell you that in negotiation, the first person who talks loses. Remember that:

"The first person who talks loses."

Learn to be comfortable in the silence. Take your mind off the sale for a moment and allow your partner to consider or mindfully process your offer or question. Human nature sets in, and we often speak because of this silence. You are a professional. You are the individual that must adjust and grow. Not the customer. As it happened, the salesperson may have said many facts, figures, stats, and numbers, hopefully leading to the sale in a short span of time. I use the term "at 100 mph." The salesperson is speaking quickly, going 100 mph, and the customer is listening at 20 mph. It may take a few moments of silence for the customer's brain to catch up. Allow the silence and enable the customer to mentally process everything that was said.

The salesperson must shut up and permit this to unfold. Multiple rapid-fire questions are a sure sign of nervousness. This shows low self-esteem or a lack of confidence. An experienced professional will ask a question and WAIT for an answer.

How long do I wait for an answer?

<u>As long as it takes!</u>

Silence is your friend.

Be my friend. Be quiet.

This is where the term "talking yourself out of the sale" happens. I am sure you are picturing that person you know who never shuts up. That one person who just loves to hear him/herself talk.

One day, I was working at the dealership with a salesperson. I had given this particular Kia salesperson some one-on-one training. I told him specifically what to say. Simple phrase and ask for the sale. I told him to shut the F-Up until he heard a response. The story unfolded. He met the client and did exactly what I told him to do. Then, I noticed that he bit his lip in wait. His overbite was noticed by everyone. After what felt like time stood still, seconds felt like minutes (you know what I mean), the customer asked him a follow-up question.

He followed his instructions perfectly, repeating exactly what I told him to say. He then bit his lip again. From about ten feet away, I watched this scenario unfold. The customer proceeded to converse with his wife and the sales team, and I stared at the salesperson. It was painfully obvious he hated not being able to engage with the customer, but he did, to his credit, continue to bite his lip in angst.

To only one person, the salesperson, "surprise." the customer accepted his proposal and purchased the additional products. He became a believer. This was the beginning of his "Sales" career. I think his mind was blown because of how speaking less makes the few words spoken much more powerful.

Speaking Less makes the spoken word much more powerful.

Keep quiet and allow the customer to make a decision on your question.

Four Types of questions

There are four types of questions the professional can ask the customer. They range from simple rapport building to closing-the-sale questions. Questions will allow the salesperson to gain information. Some questions build awareness, and other questions provoke the customer to realize the importance of the concern.

The four types of questions are:

1. **Conditional** – These types of questions build rapport. They help you gain information.
2. **Concern** – These types of questions are asked to build awareness of the problem.
3. **Consequence** – These questions provoke the interviewee to realize the importance of the problem.
4. **Close** – These types of questions help the customer to say yes to solving the problem.

The Art of PASS - FAIL

Conditional Questions – Rapport Building

1. How are you?
2. How do you like your car?
3. What did you do this weekend?
4. How do you drive your vehicle?
5. Do you tow a boat?
6. Do you like to sail?
7. Do you like to run ultramarathons?
8. What is important to you in a shoe?
9. What is your favorite color?
10. How long have you worked at your job?
11. What are the features you are looking for in a home?

The point of these questions is to get the customer into rapport. The salesperson and the customer are having a conversation. The service professional is hopefully learning valuable information about the customer. These questions are not just reserved for objection handling. These types of questions are asked during all aspects of the customer interaction process. Many inexperienced salespeople focus on the conditional questions instead of probing further. Buyers quickly become bored if asked too many conditional questions. It is important to understand the different types of questions and how they help the salesperson move the sale forward. Asking questions provides a useful understanding and builds a connection with the customer.

Concern Questions – Awareness

1. Are you aware that transmission fluid, like oil, requires service at regularly scheduled intervals?
2. Are you satisfied with the performance of your running shoes?
3. Has your television given you the reliability you are looking for?
4. Are you aware that continuing to avoid the dentist is going to add to the cost of future dentistry and could increase disease?
5. Are you aware that the FAA has issued a bulletin about seatbelt usage on the plane?
6. Are you aware that your actions could cause penalties or fines in the future?
7. What do you like about your current doctor?
8. How long have you been in your current relationship?
9. How much of a discount are you looking for from this product?
10. How much time do you have available?
11. If I were able to do _____, would that be of interest to you?

The Art of PASS - FAIL

Concern questions build awareness of a problem for the customer. This helps create the need for the object of your sales. The point of a concern question is to increase awareness and to build the case for the item that requires attention. Often salespeople stop here. They introduce the problem and hope the customer will purchase. Sometimes awareness is not enough. It is important to take the next step and introduce consequences.

Consequence Questions – Consequence

- What happens if you _____?
- Do you feel you will get the safety, performance, reliability, and protection you are looking for by ignoring the concern?
- Can you imagine how much time you will spend looking for a second opinion?
- Just out of curiosity, how many times per year do you go to the doctor/dentist?
- Are you aware of the consequences of not doing this?
- Are you aware of the cost of not taking care of this now?

Experienced salespeople move quickly to the consequences. Asking more consequence questions often moves the customer to the solution on major sales.

Consequence questions make the problem bigger. Making the problem larger is creating a larger need. If the need is great enough, the sale becomes easier. Sometimes these questions are difficult to ask. Confidence will allow the professional the certainty to use the consequence question when the time is right. The point is to learn how and when to use the tools in the toolbox. Once the need is so great, the customer is ready to buy, and the salesperson can move in for the close.

Close Questions – Close

- If I could show you how to save money and get this item handled, would you be interested?
- Would you like to take care of this vital service now?

Professional salespeople ask for the sale when the buyer is ready to purchase. Always ask for the sale. There are many closing techniques with options such as the "either/or" and "close." We have this and that. Which one do you prefer? This, too, is an additional type of question. The point is that by asking the right question at the right time and escalating the conversation from conditional or rapport-type questions into concern, consequences, and closing, you are guiding the customer to the solution.

The Art of PASS - FAIL

The reason customers stay open is that you set yourself up as their partner in the solution. These questions are not pressuring; they are looked upon as guidance to the proper conclusion.

8

Step-By-Step - Determine Solution

Salespeople are natural problem solvers. That is what salespeople do best. The problem is that salespeople often rush to solve the problem, and that can turn off a customer. Determining a solution is the easy part of objection handling. When a salesperson jumps to a solution after being told "NO," the customer can get offended, or worse, feel like they are a typical salesperson advisor is just a salesperson. The customer feels like the salesperson just wants to make a sale and doesn't have their interest at heart.

The LEAD approach puts determining a solution as the last step. This is frustrating to the salesperson because the *hurry up and sell* mentality is the way of life on the sales floor.

The better way is to truly LEAD a customer to solve their own concern by asking questions and setting the stage for a solution.

Determining a solution

This is agreeing to the best path. That path can be the original proposed item, or it could be a different option that was posed in the process. The best part is when both the sales or customer advisor and the former nuisance WIN. This win is what both parties are seeking. The customer gets exactly what they want because they agree to the solution. This solution is prescribed by both parties. Obviously, there may be compromise from one side or the other or both. The solution was reached by two sides coming together as one partnership. The partnership determined the solution, which led to a win for everyone.

Direct Approach - Consequences

In chapter eight, I proposed a question relating to consequences. The direct or consequence approach generally relates to money. This direct approach will work for the bold. There are times when our client or nuisance is refusing all measures. There are times when our potential buyer has a one-track mind. That mindset is to save as much of their money and possibly spend more of yours.

If a customer has a one-track mindset and sees any expenditure as a no-go solution, here is an awesome approach. I call it "consequences." Some like to lessen the approach and use the word "cost" instead. You may substitute the word cost where I use consequence. It takes the statement down a notch. The word consequence conjures up all types of memories, mostly from parents. Think back to your childhood and remember your most feared statement.

There will be consequences for doing (or not doing) this particular action.

Your eyes just widened. Your breath stopped for a moment. Your heart begins racing at the thought of your next action. Do I have your attention now?

Occasionally, in a sales presentation scenario, the potential client is only paying half attention. Yeah, Yeah, Whomp, Whomp, Whomp, Charlie Brown Christmas comes to mind. Lucy is not paying attention to Charlie. The words are not even resonating. Are we done yet? Next. Dropping the consequence bomb is a great way (at the right time) to grab the attention of the prospective buyer or nuisance.

The key is to know how to use the C word effectively.

> Are you aware of the consequences of not doing this (insert your product or service here) now?

I promise you will have the prospective customer's or nuisance's attention for a few seconds. As the potential buyer gazes inquisitively toward you, taking a break from their phone and social media activities, your next words will make or break the deal.

Are you aware of the consequences of not brushing your teeth? asked Mom. *OH S%*T!* your brain responds.

Are you aware of the consequences of buying that Red Ryder BB gun? You will shoot your eye out.

You have the prospective buyer or nuisance's attention for a few seconds. Use it wisely. This is not the time to regurgitate old ideas or some company talking point. This is the moment to lead with the most vital piece of information in your toolbox. This information is MONEY!

Experts will tell you the fear of loss is a greater motivation than hope for gain. Human nature tells us that winning $100 is nice. It also tells us that losing $100 stinks. The chance of winning is nice, but losing is ten times worse.

If you want to motivate a salesperson, give them $100. Get a commitment to make a sale, or else you will take the money back from them. The moment the money changes into the salesperson's hands, it now belongs to them. And most likely, it is already spent. This is the concept of FEAR of LOSS.

Promise to pay someone the same, or more, $100 if they complete the exact task. It becomes a mediocre request. If you do this, then it is called HOPE for GAIN.

The salesperson may come up with all the negatives for getting additional money, including the tax event that could happen.

The ultimate motivation is called fear of loss. Have you ever wondered why gamblers who lose continue to play? There are scientific reasons and lots of big words like dopamine and brain chemicals that others can cite. The bottom line is that the chemical reaction in a gambler's brain is more powerful during a loss than those produced during a win. Fear of loss is the most powerful motivator in human nature. This is the premise of creating a need.

The most powerful need is money. In my automotive classes, I instruct my students about this need. If a customer gives an objection, and you cannot get them to buy based on what they are saying, the objection is money. The customer just does not want to say it to you. I tell my students in class that if they tell you it is not about money, they are lying to you. If, at first, you don't succeed, it's about money. When money is the objection, then consequences are the solution.

Are you aware of the consequences of not buying today?

The consequences are money. The consequence of this objection is not some long-winded diatribe about all the things that could go wrong. The consequences are not about how it could cost more. The consequence is not that it could cost a lot more. How about ten times more? "NO!" The consequence is that today, the product or service costs x amount of dollars, and soon the cost will be x times ten amount of dollars. Be direct. Be specific.

Let me explain with an example. Today your investment is $100. In the very near future, the cost will be $1000. The words to use are the actual dollars and cents cost. There is an investment today of $100. If you wait, the cost to you could be $1000. The point is to lead with the money. Lead the conversation with the dollar value of today versus later. Your potential customer cares about money. Talk about money. I know how the so-called experts tell you to go build value, and when value overcomes cost, the transaction will be successful.

Right (sarcastically). If you have not built value in your product yet, hang it up. You missed this opportunity. Your chances are slim.

It is not politically correct to talk about money. Whatever. You say you are not comfortable discussing money. OK. Get another gig. Becoming the best in your industry is about overcoming your fears. Do what others refuse to do. Talk about the pink elephant in the room.

Lead the conversation with the most important item to the prospective buyer or objector. Yes, I am going to say it like this: hit them right between the eyes. Advise the customer in your most confident voice, sitting up tall, that the consequence will be this specific price.

Be comfortable talking about money.

If you perform this confidently and directly, your customer will thank you for the information. They will either recognize that you are providing additional information and buy from you, or they may ask you for more information. Now, you are free to engage and show off all your knowledge of the product and the additional costs for the client.

I get told this could be offensive to the prospective client. I dismiss that as a salesperson's fear. Whether you have a five-minute or five-year relationship with the prospective buyer, they need all the information to make an informed decision. The job of the salesperson or customer service professional is to be a conduit of information. Some of that information is the significance of not doing something. A prospective buyer would rather know from you the consequences of waiting versus finding out later and having an added direct expense. Then, they'd get the upper hand by stating, "You never told me!"

As the salesperson, you are the product expert. This could be in manufacturing, automotive, auto-related sales and service, dentistry, medical sales, insurance, or any other field.

I recently rented a car at a national chain rental agency in Chicago at O'Hare Airport. The story goes that my flight was being canceled due to snow, and I needed to get to my destination by the next morning. Now, if you are not familiar with the roads and drivers in Chicago, use your imagination. This is a snowy, rainy day. There

The Art of PASS - FAIL

is enough snow coming down to cancel flights in a city where snow is normal. It is Chicago!

The drivers, as far as I am concerned, are not polite to start with. The directions and roads are complicated to navigate, especially for a person who lives on an island. A busy day on our island is when two cars show up in the traffic circle at one time.

So, I showed up at the rental agency without a reservation. On the rental agency app, I can make my selection for the type of car and other products available. This includes the agency favorite, the collision damage waiver (CWD). I, in fifteen years of travel, have yet to select this item. (Did I say that out loud?) I do have a nationally recognized auto insurance brand, and I am covered in the event of an accident. As this day unfolded, the representative did something unexpected.

> *Mr. Shaw, we have you set up for a brand-new Chrysler 300. It will be in the executive aisle. Last question? Would you like the CDW?*
>
> *"NO,"* I laughingly smiled and stated. *I never get that but thank you,* I replied

politely. I do like the "would you like fries with that" presentation, though.

Next, the representative blew my mind with her question.

Mr. Shaw, are you aware of the consequences of not taking the CDW?

Yes, yes, I replied.

She said, *This new 300 cost over $50,000, and you would be responsible if something happened in the SNOW and RAIN on the way to your destination.*

I paused for a moment and pictured the crazy drivers in Chicago on the expressway and the surrounding downtown area.

Hmmm, so if I buy the CDW, then I am not responsible in the event of a crash?

She replied, *Yes, Sir. We take care of everything.*

The Art of PASS - FAIL

My entire body, mind, and being sighed in relief. I am off the hook all the way to Iowa.

YES, please sign me up for 20 bucks or whatever the cost. Fear of Loss.

Listen, I do have a great job, car insurance, and such. Why would I place myself in a position for the responsibility and liability for a $50,000+ automobile when there is an option for someone else to take that burden? I certainly did not need the headache and or the points on my insurance because of the unknown in the next few hours. My fear of loss kicked in, and I happily purchased the CDW.

No, I did not have an accident! As I drove highway 94 north out of town, cars were slipping and sliding; some were not even in the proper lane. Who would even know where the lanes are? It was so nasty outside. The best part of the story is that as I noticed the vehicles on the side of the road on the shoulder and nearby ditches, I released my death grip on the wheel, eased my way to the center of the road, and cruised into Iowa with not a care in the world. Thank you for presenting me with the consequences. My peace of mind was well worth the extra $20.

The phrase "Are you aware of the consequences?" is probably one of the most powerful expressions or tools in our vocabulary toolbox. It certainly brings up memories of a parental figure in our past. Whether it's brushing your teeth, sipping that beer, or dating that boy or girl, the next actions you take will result in some sort of parental expression of love, mentoring, or possible beating. Similarly, the resulting look from the potential client will be priceless. Use this captured moment of attention wisely. Utilize every tool in your personal toolbox as you speak. Capture the LE in LEAD with your body language and tone as you deliver the C or Consequence word. Ensure the potential client is aware of your positive nature and good reasons for using this approach.

Collect your big fat commission check in the end.

10
Return Policy

To fully maximize your company dollars for this book, we most likely need to discuss the return policy of your company. Does the company have a policy, and is it clear? Does it state how and why a customer can get a refund? Is it open-ended for a customer service representative (CSR) to decide? What if my meal takes too long or my drink tastes bad? Can the waiter, server, or bartender make a customer decision? I am not going to tell you that one bad drink means the whole crowd gets a free round. I am not even going to tell you that poor service means that the customer gets a discount, something free, or any of that nonsense. I am not here to tell you how to manage your business. You need to decide for yourself and your company how to administer your customer service. It is your company. I am only here to suggest that without a clear policy, even the best of us is just making it up as we go.

If everyone gets a refund, well, then do not argue and simply make it easy for the customer to return the item. It would appear to me that this policy is easy to administer, and everyone goes away happy. Maybe the company gets great press and sales go up because there are no unhappy customers. Please, as the business owner or associate, have a clear policy for each person to follow.

Please have your customers aware of your policy as well.

I can cite many examples of excellent customer service – return policy:

- Apple – Almost any reason. Just return it for a full refund.
- Nordstrom – We take anything back for any reason.
- Amazon Prime – No worries here, no package, "NO" problem. Refund or reorder. It is that easy.

There are many other stores that may have less-than-ideal return policies:

- Target – They make customers jump through hoops to get their money back. The last time I tried to return something at this company, they gave me a test to verify my story. The darn juicer just broke. The salesperson, I believe, was trained to make it so frustrating that the consumer would give up. I did. Never to return, either. Did I mention I am a Target nuisance consumer?
- Car Dealerships – Ha! What is a refund? These folks will always find a way not to give your money back and determine another cause for the original concern.
- Insurance Companies – Can we find reasons not to pay a claim?

Most of those are my humble opinions from experience while shopping at well-established retailers. Trust me. I am always on the lookout for the best experiences to share with my clients and associates. Are you?

The idea is to be clear with customers as well as employees. Once the policy is clear, the associate can then work toward living up to the standard. The next step is to train associates to that end. It is important that customer service associates are well-versed in the company standards and can begin to make decisions based upon real principles.

The Art of PASS - FAIL

I could write for days about doing what is right for your customer. I can write volumes. In fact, volumes have already been written on how to take care of customers. I leave that for the others. My role is simply to give you, the company or the company representative, the tools you need to defuse the customer so that an amicable solution can be reached. My role is also to provide the true salesperson with a simple tool to guide the customer to a "YES" conversation. ***I will get you there.*** Your mastery of the process will determine the final fate.

If you are inclined to say this stuff is bunk, please stop reading now! Throw the book out. Heck, ask me for a refund. I can appreciate your apprehension and would like to ask you to trash the book or give it to someone who cares about improvement. I am not writing here to reason with you. I am not writing this book to have you tell me this will not work in your organization.

You are right! It will or it will not. Either way is satisfactory to me. The thousands of other high-performing sales and customer service professionals will continue to kick your butt with simpler lives, less stress in the workplace, and greater income! Or you too can make more money!

11

L.E.A.D.
Customer-Handling Management

In the previous chapters, I made the case for utilizing LEAD as the primary approach in objection handling. Here I would like to demonstrate this approach with a nuisance customer. The premise of this chapter is to show how LEAD can be used in various scenarios.

Listen – Restate – Acknowledge
Empathize – Align – Partner
Ask Questions – Gain Permission
Determine Solution – Agree to Best Path

Often, when a customer comes into our place of business, they can be frustrated with a product and need

The Art of PASS - FAIL

help. Other times, customers come to our place of business, and we can cause them misery. In either scenario, LEAD will serve you well.

Let's examine the first scenario. A frustrated customer comes into a retail establishment. The product that was purchased is not working as designed. I use "frustrated" as a polite term, as many will be over-the-top angry. Sometimes frustrated or angry customers can swear or use foul four-letter words. The customer often feels as if they have power over the business when they are loud in our waiting rooms or in front of other guests. That is great. Allow the customer to have the power. Allow the customer all the power or control they feel they need. They are the customer. A well-trained professional does not need to hide in an office or out of sight from others.

The talent and skill are for the professional to use the tools in front of others so that they all become ambassadors. All companies make mistakes. The art is to turn a dissatisfied customer into an envoy of the company. LEAD will do that.

I hear many individuals say that they will not tolerate another person yelling and especially cursing at them. They are offended by foul language. I even hear professionals telling a customer to stop cursing. I have seen others even walk away from irate people. My goal is not to offend; however, this just shows the lack of training. If a customer is mad and the representative cannot defuse them, or worse, begins yelling back, interrupting them, or hanging up on them, it is not going to solve ANYTHING.

If you yell at a nuisance, they will get louder. If you tell a nuisance to stop cursing, they will curse more. If you hang up on a nuisance, the next person who answers the phone is going to enjoy an even more escalated extremist. An extremist will cause your company damage: not physical, but time and monetary damage. This extremist will damage your social media reputation as well as any other means they can to cause you harm. Instead, be confident, lower your tone so as not to threaten, and defuse the nuisance.

I was once a Target store's extreme customer nuisance. In a training session, I was discussing consumer behavior, and I spent five minutes talking about how I was an Apple store ambassador. I then spent twenty additional minutes persuading my seminar of students, who were high-level executives, why not to shop at Target stores. Some of the executives thought I rambled aimlessly about why I disliked the store. The bright ones realized this was not a wandering rant; it was a well-thought-out, well-placed subliminal message.

Your ambassador will deliver a message of goodwill. Some will even promote you to their friends and sphere of influence. Your nuisance extremist will make sure that everyone they encounter knows what a piece of crap you are. Does that offend you? Then learn how to defuse the nuisance. Make them an ambassador. I did not shop at Target for a good ten years after my incident. The internet blogosphere once noted that it takes about twelve positive reviews to overcome one negative review.

The point is to master the art of customer management. All companies make mistakes. Ensure that you, as the customer service professional, get a chance to handle that nuisance. Master this skill and LEAD your customer to the best outcome for both of you.

Since we are discussing the extremist, why not just deal with one now? The nuisance walks into a bar, and the bartender says... HA! This is "NO" joke.

Example Situation

One Tuesday afternoon, a traveler dropped his laundry off at the hotel lobby concierge. The hotel, in conjunction with the local cleaners, has a relationship and promises to launder the hotel guests' clothes in one day. The guest drops off before 8 a.m., and the clothes are returned by 5 p.m. This is standard hospitality practice.

This time, the clothes were not returned to the traveler on Wednesday by 5 p.m. As would most, the traveler had dropped his clothes off a day early in anticipation of any problems. Business travelers are smart that way. The laundry service claimed the clothes would be returned the next day, and all would be well. As you can imagine, the clothes never arrived on Wednesday. On Thursday morning, the traveler contacted the laundry service through the hotel to investigate. Here is the first part of the conversation:

Business Traveler: Hello, yes, my clothes have been missing now for 2 days. When are they going to be returned?

Laundry Person: I'm sorry for the delay; we will be over in the morning at 10 a.m. with your clothes.

Business Traveler: (Elevating his tone) 10 a.m. is too late. I work all day and have a flight to catch afterward.

The Art of PASS - FAIL

Laundry Person: I understand. We are about five miles from the hotel, so with traffic, it will take us until then to deliver.

Business Traveler: I do not think you do understand. You have had my laundry for two days now, and I need my clothes.

LP: I understand, but it is after 5 p.m. now, and we do not have a way to return them to you.

BT: I do not think you do understand.

LP: I do understand; you need your clothes.

After a heated exchange of words, the Business Traveler was growing increasingly upset with the Laundry Person.

BT: Are you a frequent traveler?

LP: "NO."

BT: Do you hop on a flight every Sunday and Thursday?

LP: "NO."

BT: Do you pack a minimal amount of clothing and travel the world for a living?

LP: "NO."

BT: If your underwear is not washed and cleaned tonight, does it really matter to you?

LP: "NO."

BT: Are you catching a flight tomorrow at 4 p.m.?

LP: "NO."

BT: Have you ever flown around the country without your dress clothes or underwear?

LP: "NO."

BT: THEN YOU DO NOT UNDERSTAND! STOP TELLING ME YOU UNDERSTAND MY SITUATION! GET ME MY F-ING CLOTHES!

LP: Well, there is no need to curse!

Click!

The Art of PASS - FAIL

What happened here is exactly what happens every day in the real world. The business performs its normal operations, or they fail trying to perform normal activity. In this circumstance, the business failed. The business continued to fail by its improper handling of the situation. The business failed by trying to SAY they understood. The cleaning person claimed they understood. Once it was pointed out to her that they did not understand, they collapsed. They failed again.

I could share a chart of anxiety on a scale of one to ten. What is the point of a chart that identifies the level of anxiety? The customer either buys from you or does not. The customer continues to be your customer or does not. The customer is happy, or the customer is not happy. The situation is a PASS or FAIL situation. If the customer feels the business has failed, the customer may take whatever action they feel is justified. The action can be as simple as filing a complaint with the company, filing a complaint on the internet or on social media, demanding money back, or more.

I can compare this to an oil leak in your car. Well, it is kind of leaking. Kind of Leaking? Or is it actually leaking? When a chef puts a cling-tight wrap on a dish, one of two things happens. Either the cling-tight wrap works or PASSES, and the food stays fresh, or the cling-tight FAILS, and the food eventually spoils. This is the exact same situation in customer service. The service passes the customer's expectations, or it fails the customer's expectations. SIMPLE!

Imagine your product. The product works up to the expectation of the customer, or it does not. If the product works as designed, that does not necessarily mean that it passes. If a customer makes a purchase and the product does not live up to the hype, or the food is not as good as the reviews, the customer becomes disappointed. I make the argument that it has FAILED. Certainly, it has failed to live up to the expectations.

Today, customers are either on your side or not. Customers choose your product or service, or they choose someone else. Customers are less forgiving today with their dollars and time. Take care of me, GREAT! Treat me bad, BOMB!

Are you a small-business owner? The only measure of success is the patron returning for another purchase. In fifteen years of training and development, I personally have never asked a client "Are you happy?"

Weak!

The Art of PASS - FAIL

What could I have done better? WEAK!

What did you think of my performance? WEAK!

The only measure of success or passing is for the client to return.

When your significant other makes dinner, do you go back for seconds? PASS. Be careful. Men, always take small portions so you can go back for more.

Let's make customer service easy. Let's make overcoming threats easy. Being a leader in customer service and sales can be difficult, so master the LEAD approach.

Example 2

In this example, a consumer has taken their car to an auto repair facility. The facility has contracted to perform multiple repairs on the vehicle. The repairs were completed, and the customer has driven away. The customer is gone for three days, and the exact same problem recurs. Let's just say it is a running condition problem. The light came on the dashboard and alerted the customer to return to the shop.

Customer: I was just here three days ago, and my light is back on.

Repair Shop: I am "sorry" that happened. Can you give me some time to figure this out?

Customer Elevated Voice: More time? You had my car for a whole day, and now the light is back on. I am not paying for anything.

Repair Shop: We will get it right into the shop and have it looked at.

Customer Elevated Voice: I am not paying for anything. I need a car to drive.

Repair Shop: Please wait while I call the rental agency to get you a car.

Customer Angry: I have already waited for twenty minutes; I am not paying for this. Fix my car.

Repair Shop: We will take care of the rental car and let you know about the repairs.

Customer: I need my car fixed ASAP, and I am not paying for anything.

The Art of PASS - FAIL

Repair Shop: We will call you as soon as we have it diagnosed.

Customer: I am calling the Better Business Bureau.

Repair Shop: Please, we are "sorry" this happened. Give us time, and we will get this figured out.

Customer: Fine.

Repair Shop: I am "sorry."

Why is the customer service representative apologizing? They are just trying to sweep the problem under the rug and move on.

The customer's attitude keeps escalating and becoming more and more frustrated. The service representative continues to TRY to help the customer, yet the customer is less happy toward the end of the conversation than at the start.

Notice that the customer stated the same thing over and over. The customer needs his complaint to be acknowledged. The service person continued to ignore what the customer was saying.

Who cares about your worthless "sorry"? Yes, your "sorry" is worthless at this time. Your "sorry" is an offer to move on. I am "sorry" (for you) this happened. I am "sorry" (that I am the one helping you) in this situation. I am "sorry" (my repair did not last.) I am "sorry" that I got caught. Can we just move on?

How many times have you been given a "sorry"? How many times today? When was the last time your spouse said "sorry"? When was the last time they meant "sorry"? A "sorry" at this point is simply a way to placate the customer. This is the representative hoping the customer will not be furious. Heck, most people just feel like saying "sorry." Many just say "sorry" even when they are not wrong.

An insincere "sorry" means nothing to the customer. A "sorry" is like telling someone to kiss off. A "sorry" at this point is like a stop sign for the representative. To the customer service agent, we feel like the "sorry" is the ultimate submission. We give up. You're right! Unfortunately, to the customer, a "sorry" is like being blown off. In customer handling, a "sorry" is a cop-out. It is an opening for the customer to escalate again.

Please note there can be a real situation where a sincere apology is necessary. Normal customer service issues are not that time. Earlier, we discussed when and where ONLY to offer a gesture of regret.

Customer communication can be learned, developed, and mastered.

> Customer communication is an art.
> Customer communication is a skill.
> Customer communication takes practice.

This is the entire premise of the book. Many people run from customer communication. Many are scared to communicate properly with their customers. I am here to share that communication with a less-than-happy customer is the difference between good and great.

It is the difference between loyalty and leaving. It is the difference between an average paycheck and a big fat paycheck. The difference between others' advice and mine is this: I am making this incredible tool available to you with three simple phrases. This is a process to master. As you master this process, you will see how customers in nearly every situation can be easily communicated with by defusing the situation, aligning with their goals, clarifying any obstacles in those goals, and setting forth a solution that works.

Remember, a customer is either in the state of Happy/Pass or Unhappy/Fail. It is your job as the product or service specialist to identify the state of mind (Pass/Fail) and keep the process moving in a positive direction. Failure to do so can easily escalate the customer into a highly anxious state of mind resulting in complaints, returns, social media destruction for you and your company, or possible litigation. Ultimately, you either keep your money or you lose your money. You pass, or you fail.

In any customer product or service situation, any time you are dealing with a customer issue or problem, there is a solution. The previous chapters lay out specifics of how to get solutions. The key point of this entire book is to develop a process to solve EVERY Situation. My background is in the automotive industry. I have overcome many normal and sometimes abnormal problems, issues, and objections. It is not because I know the solution. It is because I know a process to lead the customer to "yes." I can lead you to the answer you want. I can direct the conversation in any direction by asking the right question.

By knowing the proper process, any individual can first defuse the customer. It is most important to allow the customer to defuse themselves. A customer service representative (CSR) cannot resolve a problem when the customer is still escalating. A customer will not let you solve the problem if they (their problem) have not been acknowledged. This is the first step. Listen to the customer to hear their concern, complaint, or issue with the product. The idea is to listen to recognize the customer. We heard as children that we have two ears and one mouth. So, listen two times as much as you speak. That is great advice. The CSR is not listening to respond. The CSR is listening to ensure they fully grasp the full extent of the situation. The CSR must hear, see, and feel exactly what the real problem is from the customer.

The customer, too, must be allowed to speak. The customer must be allowed to speak in their own language. This language may be Spanish, or it may be profanity. That means a few foul, choice, spirited, and colorful words may be used to verbalize the sense of the problem. The heightened urgency may be brought to the CSR's attention by the number of curse words that land.

Oh, so many of you are now saying, "I do not put up with foul language" or "I stop people in their tracks when they cuss at me." I get a kick out of that. How is that working for you? Telling a person what not to do could get more expletives directed at you!

Some customers, whether highly educated or not, choose curse words to express themselves. Some people whom we consider nuisances are just everyday individuals who have become frustrated at the process. Their method of communicating is through four-letter words. Deal with it! If you press the nuisance to stop swearing at you, you run the risk again of escalating the situation.

Each one of you may have your own level of tolerance. If you have a low tolerance and want to throw the customer out because of a few choice words, well, good luck. Stop reading now. Pick up the book when you want great social media reviews. Pick up the book later when you are ready to make some money. Pick up the book when your skin thickens. You will need it to carry your big, fat, thick wallet.

We can discuss all the great reasons why it's important to the business to retain its customers. I think most of you are aware of that. For you reading this book, I assume that you would like to make a lot of money. Why waste fifteen minutes of being yelled at by the customer just to have them leave? Can you handle fifteen minutes of hell for a big check?

Once the customer has released their wrath upon you, take a breath. The customer may have given you a simple situation or the mother of all complaints. Take a moment to compose your response. Count to ten. Formulate the proper response. Create silence. You are the master of silence.

Now and only now, you may restate the customer's concern right back to them. I will let you decide if the spirited words are in your response. The step is for you to restate or acknowledge the customer's concern or issue. Your goal for this step is to have the customer agree with your summary statement. You may restate exactly, summarize, or even repeat the most important part of the customer story.

Customer: Your product is supposed to cook chicken wings in ten glorious minutes. That's what the infomercial said. Mine takes fifteen minutes or longer. This wing fryer sucks. Everything in your store sucks.

CSR: Let me see if I have this correct: you believe my store sucks, and the wing fryer sucks. The infomercial said it would take ten minutes to cook, and yours is taking fifteen minutes or longer.

Customer: YES! That is Correct! ("ssssssssshhhhhh" - the sound of a balloon deflating)

Read that again.

The CSR in the example restated nearly exactly the words of the customer. The customer and the CSR have the exact same comprehension of the problem to solve. The wind has just gone out of their sails. What is holding up the wall now? Nothing. The customer is agreeing with you that this is the problem. GREAT!

Notice two keywords that have NOT been said.

"Understand" or "Sorry"

A "sorry" is not necessary in this scenario. The CSR (you) simply listened to the customer and restated what the customer stated.

The next step is to demonstrate to the customer that you have empathy for the situation. This step is to show the customer that you are on their side. The idea is to align yourself with the customer. Often there is a non-physical wall between you and the customer. There might even be a counter, a phone, or thousands of miles between the two of you. Demonstrating empathy is the key. Yes, empathy shows your "understanding" of the situation. However, using the word "understanding" is the shortest path to a social media bomb. As a CSR, we have no idea of the behind-the-scenes situation the customer is living through. A CSR may truly have been in the exact same situation as the customer, but you never know. Avoid, at all costs, using the word "understand," and instead, demonstrate by sharing how you understand.

Here are three examples of demonstrating your empathy that may be appropriate.

If I were in your shoes. I would feel the same way...

This is what we discussed in the book. You may be an expert with empathy and add this as a bridge statement to your personality.

If that happened to me. I may not be as nice as you are being right now.

Or this added to the bridge.

> **In fact, that actually happened to me recently, and I did not handle it very well.**

Notice that as we develop empathy statements, they are not AGREEMENTS; they simply allow the customer to see you as an equal. The statements give the customer peace of mind that the two are the same or similar. The proverbial wall has gone away. You have climbed over the wall or the counter. You have closed the distance through the phone, internet, or the miles of ocean between you.

Yes, there are no more walls between you, yet there is still a problem to solve. There is still a problem, and the customer is about to allow you to begin to solve it. "Now you are solving it as an advocate, not an adversary.

Remember our three phrases to master.

L – *Listen* - If I hear you correctly ___
E – *Empathize* - If I were in your shoes, I might feel the same way.

The Art of PASS - FAIL

A – *Ask* - May I ask you a question?
D – *Determine Solution* - Comes naturally as you agree to the solution.

Maximizing your Life - Beyond the Book

Breathe in, breathe out. Relax for a moment. The last few hours you spent enjoying the read can and will change your life. It will change your life if you allow it. Process the message that comes through these pages. The key points of this work are to realize that "NO" is just the beginning. Start with "NO" and move forward step-by-step. Practice the LEAD approach on small things with your family and notice their reaction. Notice the small changes in behavior after being acknowledged.

Observe the reaction to your empathy statement. Ask for permission in a polite conversation. Subtle changes are taking place before your eyes. Be open to the discovery of a new approach. Those transformations in others' behavior are caused by your words. Your words are your power. Choose the best words and the least number of words to make your case.

Leverage your tone and body language. Your tone and actions supercharge others' conduct. Be aware of the authority you begin to wield with language. Use your new powers for good. This good is for all involved, including your family, customer, or prospective buyer.

The Art of PASS - FAIL

You have the ultimate product, service, widget, device, or software to bring about the most influence needed by others. Be confident in your newfound powers and majestically demonstrate them to others.

You are "the one," and you deserve all that comes with that distinction. Through practice and development, you are a master of words, tone, and actions. This mastery, when internalized, ultimately leads you to realize your dreams and desires. I salute your effort and your commitment.

www.ingramcontent.com/pod-product-compliance
Lightning Source LLC
Chambersburg PA
CBHW040741060526
44119CB00075B/205